Learning Without Labels

Improving outcomes for vulnerable pupils

Edited by Marc Rowland

"Grounded, relevant and uplifting"
Baroness Morris of Yardley

National Education Trust

First Published 2017

by John Catt Educational Ltd,
15 Riduna Park,
Station Road,
Melton, Woodbridge IP12 1QT

Tel: +44 (0) 1394 389850
Email: enquiries@johncatt.com
Website: www.johncatt.com

Opinions expressed in this publication are those of the contributors and are not necessarily those of the publishers or the editors. We cannot accept responsibility for any errors or omissions.

ISBN: 978 1 911382 15 7

Set and designed by John Catt Educational Limited

Contents

Introduction 7

Acknowledgements 10

Foreword: Every child should thrive in school, not just survive...... 11

LEADERSHIP **13**

On labelling children 15

What's in your schema for SEN? 18

Doing things differently: What we can learn by looking outwards...21

A Tale of Two Systems 24

We are all vulnerable sometimes 27

Learners without Labels 30

On Social Mobility Policy.. 31

"Alone we can do so little; together we can do so much," Helen Keller 37

Striving for excellence for all...................................... 39

A blank canvas: releasing the imagination for all............... 41

Recognising the strengths within 'Disadvantaged' communities and supporting those who are struggling 44

Training fleas: Why we should stop making excuses for our disadvantaged pupils... 48

No Excuses 51

PRACTICAL STRATEGIES............................... **55**

Tackling the Language Gap.. 57

Youth Work and Schools: An untapped opportunity for partnership?..60

A Pathway for tackling the unknown 63

More effective use of Teaching Assistants 70

Developing teachers to enable great learning for vulnerable pupils 74

It takes a village …to raise a child 77

Waiting for the right time to speak; knowing you'll be heard 81

Cracks in the Pavement – The Disadvantaged and University.........83

How support staff can improve outcomes for vulnerable learners ..85

Supporting struggling readers at Key Stage 3 88

Improving educational outcomes for Black, Asian and Minority
Ethnic (BAME) pupils 91

Access to the community of educated citizens: The importance of
what we learn 94

Relocation, relocation, relocation: Managing school transfer for
high mobility families 97

Young carers...100

Afterword 104

Further Reading..107

Introduction

Labelling pupils has its place. Labels can provide useful indicators for pupils who may be at risk of underachievement. Labels can mean additional funding for schools. But taken simply at face value labels can set limits on what pupils can achieve.

Having a label increases the awareness amongst education professionals that a child is vulnerable in some way. But the label alone actually tells us very little. What do we actually know about a child who is defined as 'SEND', 'Pupil Premium' or 'LAC'? It is critically important to understand pupil *need*. And these are the pupils that need the highest quality education. A great education impacts on these pupils the most. Andreas Schleicher of the OECD says *'What really distinguishes education systems is their capacity to deploy resources where they can make the most difference. Your effect size as a teacher is a lot bigger for a student who doesn't have a privileged background.'*[1]

However, even if we know more than just the label and start to understand the needs of the individuals, we still need practical solutions. We need to ensure vulnerable pupils are being supported with high quality teaching and learning strategies. Sometimes we need practical strategies to remove barriers to *accessing* high quality teaching. For example, how should schools support disadvantaged pupils who have experienced language poverty in the early years of their lives? What makes great learning for a teenage girl with autism and high levels of anxiety? How can schools effectively support struggling readers at key stage 3? How can they effectively support better mental health and emotional wellbeing? This book aims to provide some principles to work by and some practical solutions for such challenges.

In some cases, labels can be limiting and even damaging. Teachers referring to their 'low ability pupils' is commonly heard in schools. Other synonyms are no better, whether it's circles, red group, snail group or other proxies for the 'bottom set'. In my experience pupils in such groups are socio economically disadvantaged learners who haven't accessed high quality early years education, have grown up with limited access to language and cultural capital. They may not be achieving optimally at the moment, but labelling them as low ability is doing them a great disservice. Mary Myatt's opening essay tackles this issue in more depth, but we do these pupils a great disservice if we simply group them together and have them taught by the least qualified / experienced staff in an intervention group. These pupils need the highest quality teaching, the highest expectations and close monitoring.

It would be very difficult to cover every label given to pupils and try to offer solutions to all within this book. But I am increasingly convinced that there are six key features of schools that are most effective in securing excellent outcomes for their most vulnerable learners:

---

1   Rowland, M (2015). An Updated Guide to the Pupil Premium, John Catt Education Ltd

1. Strong **leadership, culture and values**, underpinned by the understanding that a great education is far more than meeting accountability targets or employability for pupils. **Sarah Wild's** essay sets out why we need to go beyond qualifications for girls with autism to be successful adults: *'Eight GCSEs are not terribly useful... if you are unable to communicate with people you don't know'.* **David Bartram** argues the same for children with special educational needs, using an international example: *'The school didn't just know the destination data of its pupils, it maintained relationships with the families and the employers, visiting young people in the workplace well beyond the school leaving date'.*

2. **High expectations** of all pupils, regardless of background or barrier to learning. Reaching age related expectations or a grade C is not enough. **Mary Myatt** sets out how well intentioned actions resulting from ability labels can lead to lower expectations. These can have a negative long term impact on pupil outcomes: *'We do not truly know what anyone is capable of until they are given interesting and difficult things to do'.*

3. A clear understanding of the **barriers to learning** vulnerable learners face. A focus on the importance of good adult – pupil relationships. And a relentless drive to overcome barriers. Never blaming pupils or families. A recognition that many learners may be vulnerable even if they do not meet the criteria for a particular label. **Kate Atkins** highlights the language deficit as a key barrier, and offers some thoughts about how to overcome language poverty early: *'I want adults to provide a running commentary for play activities.'* **Rob Webster** does the same for highly mobile learners: *'Transient pupils are not guests to be hosted before moving on again'.*

4. **Targeted strategies** that prioritise access to the highest quality teaching and focus on pupil need. Interventions evidence based. **Martina Lecky** sets out a whole school, evidence based strategy that focuses on early intervention and class teachers being accountable for the outcomes of disadvantaged learners: *'Disadvantaged pupils have the most effective teachers'.* **James Hollinsley** provides a framework for how schools can help support better mental health for primary pupils: *'Provide a place to talk and feel protected'.*

5. A **reflective, evaluative culture**, where data and evidence is used intelligently for improvement. As **David Bartram** points out, in 2014/15, there were 11,970 fixed term exclusions in year 6 nationally. In year 7 there were 33,100. Pupils with special educational needs are disproportionately represented in these figures. **Sean O'Regan** says the most vulnerable pupils are like the canary in the coal mine. If the system goes wrong it will hit them first.

6. A recognition that the highest level of accountability is to pupils and their families. Where that sense of accountability for all pupils is shared across the school, from governors to midday supervisors. **Amanda Jennings** sets out how to secure whole school accountability for every learner in her essay: 'School culture does not happen by chance or mistake... It is tenderly

nurtured, honed and developed so that no matter *what or who is being scrutinised, the message 'we can succeed' remains unmistakable'.*

Vulnerable learners: why we need to do better...

- Just 14% of looked after children achieved five good GCSEs including English and Maths (2015)

- Just 7% of care leavers go to university. Fewer than 1% of all children are in care, but they make up two fifths of children in secure training centres or young offender institutions

- 6% of 16-64 years olds with learning disabilities are in work. The figure is 5.2% for females

- 46% of people entering the prison system have literacy skills no higher than an 11-year-old

- Fewer than 44% of disadvantaged pupils achieved five good GCSEs including English and Maths in 2016

- Boys account for 97% of the 829 children in custody in England and Wales in September 2016

- 12% of children in secure training centres said they were Gypsy, Roma or Traveller, nearly 100 times greater than the estimated proportion in the general population

- Approximately 200,000 children had a parent in prison in 2009. There is no official record keeping of whether prisoners have a child under the age of 18.[1][2]

John Bird, Founder of *The Big Issue,* said '*When I learned to read at the age of 16 I suddenly got in touch with education, with the chance of becoming a different kind of boy. Not the one always in trouble with the police, but someone who in the end make the most of myself. Get behind literacy and you get behind social justice and social opportunity*'

A great education creates opportunity and choice. Our education system can be deemed successful if it creates achievement and opportunity for all, whatever the challenges pupils face, whatever labels they are given. This book aims to make a small contribution to helping that happen.

Marc Rowland, March 2017

---

2   www.prisonreformtrust.org.uk/Publications/Factfile
www.bbc.co.uk/news/disability-35005362
www.gov.uk

Acknowledgements

A huge thanks to all colleagues who have contributed an essay to the book. The purpose of the publication was to try to share effective strategies and approaches to enable learning for some of our most vulnerable pupils. Everyone has found the time for this at a time when they are perhaps busier than ever.

I would like to thank my colleague Kate Cheshire, who has shown endless patience and perseverance with the administration needed to create the book. Also a big thanks to Kevin McGrath, former trustee of the National Education Trust and founder of the Clink Charity for reminding me what happens to those that the education system has failed.

The biggest thank you goes to my friend and colleague Debbie Salmon, who has been endlessly supportive with the book, but never hesitated to tell me about things I have done which are not very good. Debs' contribution has been brilliant.

Finally, I would like to thank my good friend, former education journalist, the late Mike Baker, who still inspires me to believe that most things are possible.

Marc Rowland

Foreword

Every child should thrive in school, not just survive.

Education has to be about so much more than exam results. Schools should be flexible in their approach so that every child has access to a learning environment that meets their needs, promotes feelings of safety, that encourages them, and promotes the highest expectations and ambitions for all children. With these elements in place children will finish their education as well-rounded, happy, confident individuals, able to achieve their ambitions and meet high aspirations because they believe in themselves. That is the purpose of education; to create the next generation of tolerant, thoughtful, resilient, determined and ambitious adults.

As a mum of five, I've had lots of experience of the system. Two of my children have special needs, and even as an educated parent from a relatively privileged background, it was hard to know what questions to ask and what doors to push to get the right help. For parents who did not have the support or awareness that I had, I would wonder how they would get the right help for their children; the system sometimes feels designed to keep parents out and in the dark. I have always believed that my children, all of my children, have talent and potential that could be unlocked. Often it felt as though I was the only one who believed this.

Labels can be so limiting. We as a family have faced many occasions when professionals have taken more notice of the SEND label than the child; and have limited their aspirations, expectations and hopes without taking the time to consider the young person in front of them and dream big dreams. This is the same for any educational label; for children who are socio economically disadvantaged, children who have come to live amongst us from war zones, children who are in the care system, and children who have family members in prison. Labels are often social shorthand for preconceptions and ignorance; for lazy thinking and bigotry. Educators have to see beyond them.

We were lucky in many ways. My daughter was fortunate enough to find supportive educators who truly believed every child has the potential to be amazing; people who thought outside the box, who took a chance on there being more to her anxiety-driven, challenging behaviours. These people pushed the boundaries of expectations and fought against the restrictions of a 'system' that had prevented her becoming the best she could be. They believed in her, nurtured her, persevered with her, praised and encouraged her. They re-captured her imagination, passion and interest in life, and helped her to believe in a positive future ahead.

Beth says:

"When I started at the school, I begged to do easy work believing I was incapable of much else. Thankfully the teachers had more faith in me than I did, and refused. They never once gave up on me, no matter what I threw at them, and slowly but surely I started to let them in. I gradually began to trust their firm but loving boundaries and felt safe inside them.

The turning point came when I got almost full marks for a test. I was so excited and proud and I could see that school were just as proud, as was my mum when I rang to tell her. They had believed in me and encouraged me and this result gave me the incentive to try extra hard. At the end of my first full school year, I took two GCSEs a year early and achieved A* and B! I couldn't quite believe it. The following year I gained 6 more A-C grades.

I achieved far more than I had ever believed possible. Yet, to the school and to my parents it was not such a surprise. They had always believed in me. If it wasn't through their perseverance, through trying lots of different strategies and working together until they found out what worked best, along with constant encouragement, I don't know where I would be. I think every child should have the chance to go to a school like that."

Every child is unique, and as such there can't possibly be a 'one size fits all' education system that can truly work. Through the pages of this book, perhaps a few more people will be inspired and empowered to think outside the box and be brave enough to push against walls that restrict, walls that conform to a pattern designed to fit a majority. Perhaps then, fewer children will end their school days feeling they have failed school.

Emma and Beth Mitchell. Beth has Asperger's. Emma, Beth's mum, has three children.

Leadership

Effective leadership is critical in ensuring good outcomes for the most vulnerable learners. The best leaders understand that the highest level of accountability is to pupils and their families. They set the 'tone', the 'climate' and have the confidence to encourage professional conversations and debate as part of securing a collective vision for the most vulnerable.

This section is also about Culture and Values. Without getting these right at system, school or class level the outcomes of the most vulnerable pupils are at risk. Children from more fortunate families are likely to be better equipped to cope with high teacher turnover, poorly managed transition, a lack of work experience or limited cultural capital in the curriculum.

Mary Myatt, Education Adviser | On Labelling Children | Highlighting the risks associated with grouping pupils by simplistic ability labels.

Jarlath O'Brien, Head, Carwarden House Special School | What's your Schema for SEN? | How cognitive frameworks affect our judgements and can set limits on children with Special Educational Needs and Disability.

David Bartram OBE, London Leadership Strategy | Schools that do things differently | A case study of a school that prioritises accountability to pupils and families first.

Sean O'Regan, Director, Standards and Achievement, Education Department Jersey | A Tale of Two Systems | The importance of data and intelligence, the possibilities they offer and the challenges they create.

Simon Knight, Director of Education, National Education Trust | We are all Vulnerable Sometimes | Why it is important that schools focus on great outcomes for all pupils, not just those that are the focus of government policy.

Wasim Butt, Director of Learning, Tri Borough Alternative Provision | Learners without Labels | Reimagining what's possible: How to overcome barriers faced by pupils in Alternative Provision.

Marc Rowland, Director of Policy and Research, National Education Trust | On Social Mobility Policy | Practical, evidence based solutions to improve social mobility for all.

Sarah Wild, Headteacher, Limpsfield Grange Special School | Alone we can do so little, together so much | Beyond qualifications: creating great educational outcomes for girls with autism.

Amanda Jennings, Headteacher, Ray Lodge Primary School | Striving for Excellence for All | Developing whole school accountability for vulnerable learners.

James Biddulph, Headteacher, University of Cambridge Primary School | A Blank Canvas | Creating a school learning culture based on ambition, innovation and inclusion.

Marva Rollins OBE, Headteacher, Raynham Primary School | Out of difficulty comes the seeds of possibility | Recognising the strengths within disadvantaged communities.

Kate Masters, Lead Practitioner, Vulnerable Learners, Borough of Poole | Training fleas: Why we should stop making excuses for our disadvantaged pupils | The seven building blocks for tackling educational disadvantage.

Martina Lecky, Headteacher, Ruislip High School | Avoiding bolt ons: the importance of an evidence based strategy and whole school approach to overcoming educational disadvantage.

> "Vulnerable and disadvantaged pupils are capable of much more. It should not matter if they do not get read to at home. We need to teach them! During the school day, before school, after school, on Saturdays, during the holidays. When time, space and people are limited, push, beg, borrow or bang the drum to make it happen. There is no reasons why a child from a poorer background cannot add fractions with different denominators or discuss Shakespeare's use of comedy. Disadvantaged pupils should have the opportunity to know 'what all the others know. As teachers and leaders, it is our job to make it happen, because if we don't, who will?"
>
> **Marios Solomonides, Freshwaters Primary Academy**

On labelling children

'It's very easy not to see the intelligence which is there.' Christopher Bryan

This is a sensitive topic. In every classroom there are children with different levels of prior attainment and with differing capacities to engage with the learning. However, the labelling of children through setting might be putting limits on their achievement.

What happens in many classrooms is that pupils are placed in groups which determine the level of work which they are expected to do. However these groups are labelled. However carefully the adults believe they have disguised the fact that they are given work of different challenge, children are remarkably astute at knowing what these mean. Whether they are on a table called leopards or lizards, they know what these names signify. Whether they are number ones or number fours they know that this involves different levels of challenge and expectation.

The problem comes when the labels remain stuck. Children self-identify with the level of work which is expected of them. This is not helpful for high prior attainers or low prior attainers. The high attainers see themselves a privileged, as being worthy of greater challenge and as 'more able' than others. All of which might be the case. But if they start to fail to achieve as well and they are allocated a different label to differentiate their work, they are likely to see themselves as failures. Similarly for the other labelled groups. Children who have the 'bottom' labels, and they do know they are labelled bottom, feel that they cannot tackle more demanding work. They are often supported by an adult which is often appropriate, but what sometimes happens is that they become dependent on the adult to help them, even when they don't need it.

Dame Alison Peacock in *'Assessment for Learning without Limits'*[3] provides an insight into children's views on setting: 'The 'more able' loved it; they enjoyed being the 'bright' ones and having 'special' challenges set by the teacher. They also saw working with the teacher as a negative. The middle group were annoyed that they didn't get the same work and challenges as the other group; they wanted to try harder work but they had worked out they would never be moved up as there were only six seats on the top table. The 'less able' were affected the most. They felt 'dumb', useless, they thought they would never be allowed challenges as they usually worked with the teaching assistant (some by year 5 were completely dependent on the teaching assistant to help them). This 'less able' group liked the sound of some of the challenges the top group had, but knew they would never get the chance.'

Children placed in the 'lower' groups are often offered closed response tasks – matching parts of sentences, filling in gaps, completing easy worksheets, none of which really stretches them or expects them to do much. Others, by contrast

---

3   www.mheducation.co.uk/assessment-for-learning-without-limits

are given more to do and more is expected of them. While they might have a few closed exercises in order to practice or consolidate their knowledge, they are also expected to do new things with this – constructing their own sentences, coming up with other alternative adjectives in a piece of writing, suggesting alternatives to maths problems. These children are being given more opportunities both to struggle and to gain new knowledge. The others, by contrast, have insufficient expected of them and as a result, don't make the same gains as their peers. This extends the gap in their knowledge and attainment. The paradox is that by attempting to give them easier work, such exercises can often close down their capacity and opportunity to do more.

Teachers must make sense of this in order to get all children working to their highest capacity and potential. Schools which have recognised that grouping children by ability could be a problem in promoting self-limiting beliefs at all levels have done away with the naming of tables or groups. Instead, they promote teaching to the top, rather than putting a lid on what children might produce by preparing materials which only allow them to go so far. The current trend in the teaching of mathematics in primary schools is that the whole class is taught together on the key ideas and those who need additional support are given this through guidance and discussion by an adult. Those who are early graspers work on the same material but are expected to work on aspects of greater complexity and depth.

The principle is that all children are exposed to the material at the same time. Now there will always be exceptions to this: those whose cognitive ability needs one to one support, often through pre-learning sessions so that they are able to access the material and others whose grasp is so secure early on that they need additional work to challenge and extend their thinking. But for the vast majority, the expectation is to teach to the top, provide additional support for those who need it and challenge for those who are capable of dealing with greater complexity. As a result all children are exposed to a rich and demanding curriculum.

Of course, what pupils can do well in one lesson is likely to be different in another. So while a group of pupils might grasp one aspect of learning very quickly, they might be slower to grasp another. This movement in terms of their expertise is natural. Not every child is going to struggle every time and not every child is going to race ahead every time. This is how learning works. This means there needs to be fluidity and flexibility about what they do and what is expected of them.

The philosophy of 'Learning without Limits'[4] encourages schools not to label children. Their needs and barriers to learning should be identified but this is different from labelling them. A staggering statistic from Gordon Storable in The Expert Learner showed that 88% of 4 year olds placed in sets were still there by the end of their schooling. In her TEDx talk Alison Peacock describes the school journey of one child with considerable additional needs who achieved very highly at the end of his time at school. What would have happened if she had used sets?

---

4   www.amazon.co.uk/Learning-Without-Limits-Susan-Hart/dp/033521259X

What would the outcomes have been for that child if he had been labelled? It is very unlikely that he would have achieved the same top scores in his SATS.

We do not truly know what anyone is capable of until they are given interesting and difficult things to do. A 'learning without limits' environment ensures there are interesting, thought provoking, challenging things for children to do. Alongside this there needs to be plenty of appropriate support and timely feedback. If children are engaged in thoughtful, absorbing practice there is no limit to what they can achieve.

Finally, Jonathan Bryan, born with cerebral palsy after his mother was involved in a car accident started a campaign to ensure all children with 'locked-in' syndrome were taught to read and write. It took seven years before he was able to communicate and he now spends part of each day in the local primary school where he excels at maths. He also writes poems of great subtlety and wit which are read by thousands on his blog[56] 'I can talk: a silent soul emerging'. His story is a compelling example for why it is so important not to underestimate what children can do.

This is a call to all to think about how we 'label' children and what might be hidden when we do so.

Mary Myatt, Education Adviser

Mary Myatt is an education adviser. She works in schools talking to pupils, teachers and leaders about learning, leadership and the curriculum. She maintains that there are no quick fixes and that great outcomes for pupils are not achieved through tick boxes.

www.marymyatt.com

@MaryMyatt

---

5   www.dailymail.co.uk/news/article-3671847/The-lionhearted-Locked-Boy-Lad-trapped-silence-seven-years-miraculously-finding-way-signal-say-truly-astonish-you.html
6   eyecantalk.net/media/

What's in your schema for SEN?

In Richard Nisbett's book 'Mindware' about thinking, inference and reasoning and the common mistakes we make, there's an arresting section on the **schema** concept. Nisbett describes the term *schema* as referring 'to cognitive frameworks, templates or rule systems that we apply to the world to make sense of it'. We have them for all sorts of things: "basketball" (indoors, five-a-side, holding the ball in your hands) and "football" (outdoors, eleven-a-side, kicking the ball with your foot), for example, or "packed lunch" (sandwiches, fruit, crisps) and "school dinners" (hot meal, meat, vegetables).

Schemas affect our judgement, how we behave and help us to select the appropriate behaviours for different locations and events for example how we might approach visits to the dentist, job interviews or queuing in the supermarket. These schemas develop as we mature. Toddlers don't always display the social niceties we expect of adults at a wedding or when visiting a sick relative in hospital. We expect adults to have fully formed and socially appropriate schemas. This is one reason why society broadly struggles to accept adults with learning difficulties who may not demonstrate the expected behaviours in, say, the cinema.

Object schemas are used routinely in many special schools to help students with significant learning difficulties understand and prepare for what is coming next. A pair of goggles might signify that swimming is coming up, a nappy may be used to indicate that the child is to be changed. A favourite book may signal that the next lesson is English. You can see how object schemas are used to positively influence the behaviour of children for whom a regular timetable or verbal instruction in isolation is inaccessible. Without them the child may well spend large parts of the day wondering what is happening to them, especially so if they are non-ambulant and rely on adults to get them from place to place. Imagine being pushed from room to room six or so times a day with no understanding of where you're going or what's going to happen once you get there. Imagine what that would be like if you were also blind. Using object schemas mean the child is more likely to understand what is happening next and is therefore more likely to be settled and comfortable as opposed to anxious and worried.

Nisbett explains that the influence of schemas is also true in our use of stereotypes – schemas about particular types of people. Stereotypes may initially sound like an exclusively negative thing, but it isn't so. My stereotype for "policeman" is very different from my stereotype for "Member of Parliament", "barista", "postman" or "priest". It is why we spend considerable time in special schools on communication with strangers. We don't teach students about 'stranger danger' – we have to talk to strangers to get by in life – but your relationship with a bus driver will be very different to your relationship with your doctor.

This set me thinking about learning difficulties and the people who have learning difficulties. Schemas are clearly working away in the subconscious, and have developed and evolved throughout the course of our lives.

What schemas and stereotypes do you have for the following words?

ADHD, Down syndrome, Autism, Pupil premium, Looked-after, Bottom set, SEN

Are the schemas we have for these words negative in nature? Do they subconsciously lower expectations for any children we teach who happen to be described using some of these terms? I'll give you a word that's specific to me.

Fitzgerald

I am forced to admit that this word immediately brings forth some negative thoughts and words. I wish it weren't so, but they are there. I have to consciously put them away and refocus. The word does this because I worked with a number of children from the Fitzgerald family* when I first became a teacher in a comprehensive school. All of them had behavioural difficulties.

One July, as I was handed my class lists for the following year, my eyes rested on another Fitzgerald. A fraction of a second was it all it took for me to judge this child without ever meeting them. As it turned out, this particular Fitzgerald did not experience any behavioural difficulties, nor were they actually a member of that family at all (although that should have been irrelevant). I learnt salutary lesson, but my subconscious still drags up thoughts that unchallenged would unacceptably see me prejudge a child before meeting them.

Nisbett describes an experiment carried out by psychologists at Princeton University[7] in which students made stereotypical judgements about a child based on their judgement of her social class. The experiment contended that "people will expect and demand less of [working-class Hannah], and they will perceive her performance as being worse than if she were upper middle class".

Reading that chapter a number of times and thinking deeply and honestly about the subconscious schemas that are operating in my head, I am concerned that the adverse judgements made by the students in the Princeton study are more than likely to be replicated or, I fear, magnified, by society when they hear or see the words:

ADHD, Down syndrome, Autism, Pupil premium, Looked-after, Bottom set, SEN

I fear this because I have seen first-hand how society as a whole has extremely low expectations of people with Down syndrome. I see very little expectation that children with Down syndrome will go on to paid work or live independently. Why is this?

---

7   Darley and Gross, "A Hypothesis-Confirming Bias in Labelling Effects"

I contend that schemas that limit our expectations underpin and contribute heavily to the poor life outcomes for people with learning difficulties. Confront your schemas and your stereotypes. Be brutally honest with yourself. Dig deep to uncover what your subconscious mind is saying to you about those words listed above. Do the same for the people you work with now or have in the past, who have been described by those labels or others like them. It's going to take some serious effort (I haven't taught a Fitzgerald for eleven years) before each of us individually, and then society more broadly, replaces deficit schemas with ambitious ones.

* Fitzgerald is a pseudonym

Jarlath O'Brien, Headteacher – Carwarden House School

Jarlath is Headteacher of Carwarden House Community School, a special school in Surrey. He writes regularly for the *Times Educational Supplement* and is the author of *'Don't Send Him in Tomorrow'*.

@JarlathOBrien

Doing things differently: What we can learn by looking outwards

Successful schools ensure that all their pupils, whatever their additional needs, achieve their very best. This includes gaining the skills and qualifications they will need for successful transition, further education and employment. Outcomes for children with special educational needs remain unacceptably low and are well documented.[8] It is a marker of how far our education system has to develop when only 1 in 10 children with a learning disability can expect to enter employment. When they do, these jobs are often part-time or poorly paid.[9]

And then there are the outliers: schools that do things differently. These schools are often found in the most unlikely places, where extraordinary individuals are quietly and modestly going about their work whilst at the same time bucking statistical trends.

It is not only in the UK where outcomes for children with special educational needs remain stubbornly low. In Malaysia, under 1% of children with a learning difficulty secure either part-time or full-time employment. Yet at Jalan Reko, a large secondary school in the Bandar Baru Bangi township, the majority of their pupils with additional needs enter paid employment.

So what is this school doing, with almost no funding, that is having such a significant impact on the life chances of its pupils?

Careful planning at transition points

We know that transition is a particularly vulnerable time for pupils with additional needs. For example, in England the largest incremental jump in the number of fixed term exclusions takes place in Year 7; in 2014/15 there were 11,970 fixed term exclusions in Year 6 nationally compared to 33,100 fixed term exclusions in Year 7. Pupils with SEND are disproportionately represented in these figures.[10] Planning and preparation for adulthood at Jarlan Reko starts from the moment a child transfers to secondary school.

Valuing the contribution of pupils and parents

On the day of our visit, it was the pupils and parents who led the presentations on transition to the workplace rather than the teachers themselves. Positive

---

8   O'Brien, J. (2016). Don't Send Him in Tomorrow Crown House Publishing Ltd.
9   See www.mencap.org.uk/get-involved/campaigns/what-we-campaign-about/employment-and-training
10 See www.gov.uk/government/statistics/permanent-and-fixed-period-exclusions-in-england-2014-to-2015

relationships between parents and the school's senior leadership team allowed parents to contribute meaningfully to shaping both the curriculum and the provision that their children received. The school, alongside parents and employers, worked in partnership to achieve genuine co-operation.

Working with employers

The school builds great working relationships with employers. It educates employers on the challenges that employing a young person with learning difficulties can sometimes present, but also celebrates the many benefits of welcoming people with additional needs into the workplace. The school works to reduce the stigma often associated with a disability and showcases the achievements of disabled people as positive role models.

A flexible curriculum

Every child deserves an education system that responds to their individual learning requirements. As school leaders, one of our biggest challenges is to provide a curriculum that meets the needs, wants and aspirations of all pupils and their parents.

There is significant variation in the quality of curricula for children with additional needs in England and often a lack of understanding between schools as to what an effective alternative, adapted or flexible curriculum should look like.

At Jalan Reko, the school is given the freedom to modify and adapt its curriculum to best meet the needs of its pupils. The development of life skills and a route into employment are seen as the highest priorities.

A Year 10/11 catering class at Jalan Reko, planned and delivered by a local employer.

Ambition for all pupils

Underlying all of the above is the expectation that all pupils at the school will go on to achieve the skills, qualifications or experience that they need to succeed. The school takes the time to define what success looks like for different pupils, with carefully written plans that capture what high expectations of individual pupils really means.

The school doesn't just know the 'destination data' of its pupils. It maintains relationships with the families and the employers, often visiting the young people in the workplace well beyond their school leaving date.

The school is not perfect. The headteacher and senior team were very aware that provision for children with special educational needs is not as developed and comprehensive as they wanted it to be. Yet despite the lack of funding and their limited resources, the school's ambition for every child shines through. As a result, the staff team were changing the lives of children and their families that in many respects, our current education system would give up on all too easily.

David Bartram OBE, London Leadership Strategy

David is Director of SEND at the London Leadership Strategy and is Director of SEND for Future Academies, a small family of schools in South Westminster. David was awarded the OBE for services to Special Educational Needs and Disability in the 2016 New Year's Honours list.

@DavidBartram

A Tale of Two Systems

A fundamental principle of a school is to welcome all children who walk through the door; another is to treat every child with respect and care. The commitment is given on enrolment to provide the best possible education and wider opportunities to the new pupil. This is, of course only possible by knowing the child. Information is gathered from that first home visit or enrolment meeting, or as the transition documentation is pinged over from a previous school or setting. It builds rapidly as the child enters the classroom and first interacts with their classmates, teachers and support staff. Professionals want to get straight to it: the better I know the child the better I can meet her learning needs.

Here labels can so easily creep in. Some may prove helpful ('summer born', 'newly arrived', 'diagnosed special need'), others may need testing ('middle ability', 'child in need'), others feel downright unhelpful ('difficult child', 'Jamie's brother'). How do we capture what we need to know to do our job- the key characteristics of a child- without falling into the professional trap of labelling this new arrival?

As a young teacher I was troubled by the frequent refrains of "she's EAL…" or "he's SEN", not only used as catch–all labels but ones seemingly given the infinite capacity to excuse or explain away low educational outcomes.

Over the period of my sixteen years as an inner-city headteacher, the school system in England became data-rich: tracts of pupils' information codified in terms of characteristics of the learner. Data became all-encompassing as school accountability approaches increasingly relied on achievement outcomes, including by 'group'.

We sought to avoid the perceived data-driven push to rather become sophisticated in our use of data to inform this core purpose: to provide a great education. This was especially vital as so many of the children at our school were vulnerable, with a range of disadvantages presenting the significant risk of low achievement. The characteristics of the school: 98% pupils with EAL; 35 spoken languages; 28% from refugee or asylum seeking families; 62% Pupil Premium; high mobility; considerable social deprivation and significant engagement of social care.

We knew our children well, because we had to. We sifted data to elicit that which informed our work, for example, our pupil progress meetings. We didn't define Candice by these labels, but it helped us to know that Fischer Family Trust data tells us that as a summer born African-Caribbean girl pupils like her can and do achieve this level of progress over key stage 2.

We identified those key characteristics that research and experience tell us contribute to low achievement, built the learning picture of each child and did something about it. For our school, it lay in being clear on the characteristics that impacted on low attainment. In this context what matters lay in the following: having EAL; being LAC, a recent care leaver or at risk of LAC; at School Action plus or having (then) a Statement of SEN; long leave overseas of over 4 weeks in the past 2 years; absence rates over 10%; being on the CPR; very low prior attainment; or being summer born.

I moved from inner-city headship to Jersey to be Director of Standards and Achievement. I found an island education system outside the domain of the DfE (or Ofsted) presents innumerable contrasts, although the challenges faced by schools are very similar and helpfully, children remain children. No RAISE, no SATs. Very little detailed achievement data of any sort. Moving out of headship, one misses the children of course, but it may surprise some how much one misses RAISE too. To build up reliable data sets to inform school improvement was a key challenge, especially when the assessment methodology differed so widely to that in England, whilst nonetheless having students follow a near identical curriculum and take the same GCSEs and A levels.

Having built data sets to ensure both in-year reliability and comparability with previous years and with other jurisdictions was challenging enough, but we have achieved this. To seek to use data to address disadvantage when no such data has ever been collected was another task altogether. In seeking to introduce a local version of the Pupil Premium, coming up with eligibility criteria was just one of many challenges. It's hard to look to 'free school meals' as a criteria when there are no school meals *per se*, free or otherwise.

This Island community, like many coastal areas in the UK, has significant deprivation and there are many charities actively working in the sphere of alleviating poverty, including its impact on very young children. Yet Jersey has an education service with no data on pupils' economic need, and therefore no purchase on understanding the impact of this on educational attainment.

Our education system had made the case for, and has secured meaningful funding for a local version of Pupil Premium. We have signed a ground-breaking data sharing agreement with the local government's Social Security Department and are now running 51 pilot projects in 23 schools ahead of a full launch in 2017.

It's worth considering whether in doing this we are running the risk of creating a new label, a 'Jersey premium' child? I do not believe we are. Labels serve no good purpose in the classroom. Just as the challenge in the English school system is to become 'data wise', from an established position of being data rich, in Jersey we are on the journey of building up detailed knowledge of all pupils from scratch, and particularly those vulnerable to low achievement due to disadvantage.

Whilst at contrasting starting points, the aim is the same. To thoroughly know one's pupils, understand the characteristics that matter, share this knowledge with all (staff, parents/carers, the student) and utilise all of the school's resources to meet the identified needs.

Seán O'Regan, Director Standards and Achievement, Education Department – Government of Jersey

After PPE at Oxford, Seán completed teaching degrees at Reading and London. Teaching predominantly in London, he fell into headship at 32. His leadership was recognised by the Teaching Awards and in the books 'Oranges and Lemons: life in an inner city school' and 'How to create a successful school'. From School Improvement in Camden Seán returned to his home island, Jersey, where he is Director for Standards and Achievement.

@SeanFORegan

We are all vulnerable sometimes

Our education system concerns itself with aspiring to ensure that all children have equitable opportunity. Irrespective of their background, they should have the chance to achieve and indeed attain at the same level as any other child. This aspiration, characterised variously as 'Every Child Matters', as 'No Child Left Behind', or most recently as 'Educational Excellence Everywhere' tends to focus on particular groups of children identified as being at risk of low attainment.

To achieve the required improvements within the education system, we often see the use of policy levers to try and affect change, such as the Pupil Premium. This approach has led to significant amounts of money, and attention, being focused on those children who 'qualify' for this type of support.

However, this doesn't come without risk. The early implementation of the Pupil Premium was variable, and whilst we now see higher quality and use of the funding having higher impact, there is still a degree of inconsistency.

It is also interesting to consider that the way we use language within education has evolved since the Pupil Premium was introduced. When schools or Government talk about 'Disadvantaged pupils', they generally mean children from a family with a lower income who are (or who have been) eligible for free school meals. Disadvantage has come to be defined in predominantly socioeconomic terms, but there are numerous other ways in which children can be disadvantaged – either permanently or indeed temporarily.

This is now a characterisation of disadvantage. It focuses visibly on one particular group of children. It holds schools accountable for the progress of this group through the inspection process. But viewing disadvantage purely in socio economic terms risks drawing attention away from others who are at risk of lower attainment. If we want to ensure that we create an increasingly equitable education system then it's also important to consider unintended consequences in policy decisions impacting those, and as such risk promoting inequality.

In his eloquent and thought provoking book, "Don't Send Him in Tomorrow", Jarlath O'Brien highlights the impact of having a learning disability on the individual. Catastrophically low rates of employment, greater risk of permanent exclusion from education, more likely to be living in poverty, more likely to end up in prison and likely to die fifteen years earlier than the average life expectancy. But the main investment in the education of children with Special Educational Needs or Disability (SEND) has focused on the systems which govern access to provision. Less attention has been given so far to the quality of the education on offer or indeed the impact of that education on later life. There is limited value in having world class administration if we still struggle to provide consistently good provision.

If a school performs poorly during inspection in relation to pupils eligible for Pupil Premium, they can be compelled to undertake a Pupil Premium review.

Yet no mechanism currently exists for those schools whose pupils with SEND are identified as receiving a low quality education.

Systems of accountability draw attention towards particular groups. It requires strong moral leadership to ensure that in responding to these requirements, schools do not find themselves distracted from the needs of pupils who do not fall within those groups. Failing to do so risks allowing a system to flourish where some pupils' 'disadvantage' is seen to be more important than others.

It is important that schools take a proactive approach with regard to the education of the broader range of vulnerable pupils. A school initiated review of a particular aspect of provision, or of the organisation more broadly may well yield more success in terms of driving up school performance than one a school is compelled to do as a result of a poor inspection outcome.

Reactive approaches, by their very nature, are a response to a problem that already exists. We should be aspiring to address the areas we need to develop ahead of any negative impact on the education of the children we teach.

Further, it is important not to just think of the outcomes of these types of external school Pupil Premium or SEND reviews as being specific to the children for whom they were designed. The impact of a review is not limited to those pupils categorised as such. The focused attention upon vulnerable learners can have a transformative impact on the wider school, through the consideration of values and cultures as well as specific practice and pedagogy.

We also need to be mindful of the transient nature of some vulnerabilities, the turmoil that children can be exposed to unexpectedly and the impact that it can have on them. Debates around mental health and the broader emotional wellbeing of the children in our schools highlight a perceived change in the needs of the children we work with. We need to consider the extent to which we are able to meet emerging disadvantages and vulnerabilities and what may be happening to affect the changes that we may be seeing.

School leaders need to ensure that they have the clarity of vision necessary to be able to drive improvement for all pupils, irrespective of whether the quality of what their schools offer as a result addresses the political priorities of the time.

It would be a dereliction of duty to focus only on the needs of policy, when every child deserves the very best from their education. When every child has the potential to be vulnerable sometimes.

Simon Knight, Director of Education – National Education Trust

Simon is a former teacher and school leader with extensive experience in special education, in particular the education of children with severe or profound and multiple learning disabilities, a field in which he worked for eighteen years.

He has also sat on a number of education advisory groups and executive boards, including the Independent Review of Professional Standards for Teaching Assistants, and The Teachers' Professional Development Expert Group. He speaks widely on the subject of SEND and is a feature writer for the *TES*.

@simonknight100

Learners without Labels

Learners arrive at Tri Borough Alternative Provision (TBAP) with labels. They have to in order to meet the admissions criteria. Most of these learners were labelled very early on in their school careers. Now, their respective schools have deemed them 'unfit' for the mainstream and each learner has experienced some form of permanent exclusion. Each child has a unique story to tell, yet each school has a familiar tale; they feel they have exhausted all strategies, explored all avenues and have ultimately reached the end of the line.

Learners arriving here spend time during their induction period reflecting on their past experiences. Some speak of regret and wanting to return to their mainstream schools. Others of wanting to move to another 'better' school. In reality, most will stay with TBAP where they will complete their compulsory education.

Many will have low levels of aspiration and expectations. They will have poor levels of literacy and numeracy, they will lack intellectual and cultural enrichment, they will lack family experience of further education and professional careers, they may have broken family structures and poor health. They will have spent many years being labelled as such.

I have spent a considerable number of years overseeing strategies for learners at risk of permanent exclusion. I have seen firsthand the pitfalls of the system, and the pros and cons of reintegration back into mainstream schools. Upon joining TBAP, it became clear why this alternative provision worked for so many vulnerable children. For the first time, learners were *without* labels. This is the foundation for the vision we have here. It is underpinned by three core values that permeate throughout the organisation:

- Success for learners by any means
- Precise inclusion
- Starting at great

The GCSE examination results across TBAP this summer prove that these learners can achieve high standards when given sufficient time and high-quality support. Success for these young people is non-negotiable. The fact that the majority of our learners are so vulnerable means we **must** go the extra mile. Throughout the academic year skilled staff listen to learners they seek to understand their 'journey' and difficulties in their lives which make engagement a challenge.

All teachers must teach high quality lessons backed up by the right ethos, values and support. At TBAP, the secret of constant growth is to start a new sigmoid curve before the first has petered out. There is the time, as well as the resources and the energy, to get the new curve through its initial explorations and flounderings.

Collaboration within the trust further drives improvement through:

- sharing of best research, practice and ideas
- shaping of standard operating procedures
- pooling of staff, resources and budgets

All learners are given small nudges and invitations to make the right choices, to value, to believe education is character forming. But at TBAP we focus on a new kind of character – that of the confident lifelong explorer and navigator. In doing so, we provide a context for each child's natural creativity to emerge and it stimulates a deep sensitivity to all existence.

TBAP values openness and this is seen in the quality of relationships which are built and ultimately enhance the dignity of each person. Our structures are liberating rather than constricting. We have a tolerance of failure as a commitment to forgiveness, reconciliation and learning. It stresses the growth of the individual rather than the formation of people according to a set of narrow preconceived expectations. We always value the achievements and affirm the work of every learner, unlocking the latent talent in each one.

The labels our learners joined us with must be stripped away to allow for transition to employment, further study and having a positive role to play in society. Providing the opportunity for the individual to acknowledge the past but adapt for the future is key to all we do. For our learners there is no '**good enough**'.

Wasim Butt, Director of Learning – TBAP

Science teacher with significant experience as a pastoral leader and SENCO within mainstream schools. Currently working in alternative provision as a senior teacher with responsibility for Teaching and Learning. Passionate about raising the attainment of disadvantaged and vulnerable pupils.

@LatimerTBAP

On Social Mobility Policy

Improving Social Mobility has been placed at the heart of Government Policy. To do this, we need to tackle the causes of social stagnation.

Grammar Schools are back on the agenda. But they are the mountebank of social mobility. It is not enough to leap into an entrenched position and stay there. Placard waving rallies make people feel good, but they rarely change policy. We need to be in the uncomfortable chair of decision making, rather than wrapped in the cosy duvet of vocal opposition.

If grammars do have any positive impact on social mobility, that impact will be most welcome. More disadvantaged pupils getting a place at Cambridge is undoubtedly a good thing, but it will do little to tackle the deep-rooted issues our society faces. A genuine plan for social mobility needs to be bold, politically savvy, values driven and evidence based.

Tackling the language gap we see in our disadvantaged pupils at risk of underachievement. This gives virtually every other education policy a better chance of success. The language gap and the evidence for it can be described below.

'The landmark Hart and Risley study in 1995 identified "remarkable differences" in the early vocabulary experiences of young children. Researcher and author Betty Hart described the results of their observations: "Simply in words heard, the average child on welfare was having half as much experience per hour (616 words per hour) as the average working-class child (1,251 words per hour) and less than one-third that of the average child in a professional family (2,153 words per hour)" (Hart & Risley 2003, 8). This is important because vocabulary development during the preschool years is related to later reading skills and school success in general.'

In all my experience, school-led solutions are best placed to help tackle this issue, working with children and their families to make a better start to early reading.

Maximising the Impact of Early Years

Kathy Sylva's EPPSE 3-16 project shows that 2-3 years of high quality pre-school impacts on outcomes at least to 16, particularly for disadvantaged learners.

A quick glance online shows that Early Years professionals, who need to be educated to degree level, can expect to be paid between £22,000 and £33,000 (about the same as a bus driver). A well-known recruitment website lists the requirements for an Early Years professional as follows:

- excellent communication skills;
- good listening skills;
- the capacity to learn quickly;

- excellent organisational skills;
- the ability to inspire and enthuse young children;
- energy, resourcefulness, responsibility, patience and a caring nature;
- an understanding of the needs and feelings of children;
- ability to work independently, as well as being able to work in a team;
- a sense of humour and the ability to keep things in perspective.

I'd argue that subject knowledge, a fundamental understanding of research and how to apply it are the gaping omissions here, along with the highest ambitions for all, regardless of background or barrier to learning.

Better opportunities for young people with learning difficulties

6% of adults aged 16-64 with learning difficulties are in paid employment. Of those surveyed, 65% want to work. The Social Mobility challenge is at its most glaring where the people concerned are the least likely to be heard.

We need to talk about Erin*

Erin attended Limpsfield Grange Special School in Surrey. She has Asperger's and a diagnosis of Pathological Demand Avoidance. She has entrenched mental health difficulties including significant levels of self-harm, suicidal ideation and depression, and has been under the care of a psychiatrist since she was eight years old.

Erin missed half of KS2, all of Year 8 and half of Year 9 as she was unable to attend school due to her high and persistent levels of anxiety. Erin joined Limpsfield Grange at the end of the summer term in Year 9 when she became a full time boarder.

Initially Erin was self-harming at school upwards of 30 times a day. This reduced to 0 times a day in Year 11. Her attendance for Year 11 was 98%. Her GCSE results:

English B
Mathematics C
Additional Science B
Health & Social Care A
Catering A
Textiles B
Core Science B
RE A*

I've met Erin. Like many teenagers she is stubborn and determined, bright and shy. This is what she has achieved against the odds. Social Mobility needs to work for everyone, not just 'the bright poor'.

Maximising the Curriculum

In too many cases, the Key Stage 3 curriculum remains a rather desolate place. A few weeks back, I was told about pupils with excellent reading outcomes at KS2 going into year seven and being given a recommended reading list made up of authors such as Jacqueline Wilson and Roald Dahl. These suggestions sadly lack challenge and imagination.

A chasm in the DfE's business plan is the lack of a challenging, high esteem technical education pathway. This should have literacy and numeracy at its heart which doesn't narrow opportunity. We should learn from other countries about how we could do better. It remains an afterthought.

Oracy as standard

If it were measurable, I suspect that one of the greatest achievement gaps we see in our schools is oracy and articulacy. Peter Hyman's work at School21 is an exemplar of how we can improve the life chances and life choices of disadvantaged and vulnerable learners.

Good oracy, coupled with cultural literacy should be at the heart of the social mobility agenda.

The Power of Multi Academy Trusts

We are only just starting to see the potential of Multi Academy Trusts. With support, I believe we will see some diverse and innovative models evolving that produce excellent, long term outcomes for pupils of all backgrounds.

One of the true drivers for genuine, sustainable collaboration is shared accountability. Through MATs, we can create an education system which enables the very best teachers and expert support staff to work with the most disadvantaged pupils.

The quality of teaching has a significantly disproportionate effect on disadvantaged pupils. Pupils in the poorest communities are more likely to be taught by unqualified or inexperienced teachers. They are more likely to experience high teacher turnover. They are more likely to be taught by a teacher without a degree in the subject they teach. High quality teachers are more likely to move out of the most disadvantaged communities. Effective Academy Trusts have the potential to deploy teaching resources to where they are needed most within a community.

In some communities, such as rural North Yorkshire and Northumberland, Local Authorities need to be empowered to support this agenda too.

The Pupil Premium

This has been a very powerful vehicle for improving outcomes for disadvantaged learners. We should further improve the use and impact of the funding by ensuring schools have the highest of expectations, high quality teaching and cultural literacy. The policy itself should not change. The expectations of its impact should continue. Better destinations data would help inform the use of funding. Good GCSE results only open a door for disadvantaged pupils. They need to have the expectations of themselves to step through it.

The Progress Problem

Progress is one reasonable accountability measure for schools. But for individual pupils it is **attainment** that matters. 'Expected Progress' has been one of the most limiting factors for disadvantaged pupils. As George Mallory said: *'We do not live to eat and make money. We eat and make money to be able to live. That is what life means and what life is for.'* Aiming for the bare minimum means missed opportunity and wasted talent.

Leading the way

I have yet to hear any argument for more academic selection that stands up to scrutiny. Professor Deborah Eyre says it's not possible to have social mobility and a selective education system at the same time. But that is not a reason to do nothing. If we let it, grammar school proposals could become the Gavrilo Princip of a new and completely unnecessary education divide. The school-led system should be at the forefront of the alternative.

*Pseudonym used

Marc Rowland, National Education Trust

Marc is the Director of Policy and Research at the National Education Trust. Marc also works at Rosendale primary school to support two successful research projects on metacognition and lesson study.

Marc is the author of '*A Practical Guide to the Pupil Premium*' (John Catt).

Marc has been working with the Jersey Government to implement their strategy for tackling educational disadvantage 'The Jersey Premium'. He is also the co-author of the Essex LA-funded Pupil Premium self-evaluation toolkit. He has worked with North Yorkshire, Essex, Sheffield, Hampshire and Warwickshire LAs on long projects to support better outcomes for disadvantaged pupils.

@natedtrust_marc

"Alone we can do so little; together we can do so much."
Helen Keller

I work with girls who astound me every day; who push my already sky high expectations of them; who deftly dispose of social stereotypes. They are the students at Limpsfield Grange, a special school for girls with communication and interaction difficulties, most of whom have autism; which for women and girls is still sadly a very misunderstood condition. However, we are trying our best to change that.

The girls at Limpsfield Grange would be classified as vulnerable learners in any setting. Having special educational needs makes you a vulnerable learner, and often makes you a vulnerable adult too. Being female and having special needs adds an additional layer of vulnerability. In August 2016 the United Nations reported that being female and disabled or having special needs was a double disadvantage. These women and girls were often treated as helpless objects of pity or subjected to hostility, and were excluded from enjoying their fundamental human rights and freedoms. Women with disabilities were reported to be at increased risk of physical, psychological or sexual violence, and faced multiple levels of discrimination. Often they had no social value, and were either invisible or ridiculed.

Most of the girls at Limpsfield Grange have a myriad of complex needs, which often overlap with mental health difficulties. Many of the girls live in families that are economically disadvantaged; families that have experienced poverty for generations. High numbers of our girls have been adopted from care or have experienced family breakdown and are looked after. All of the girls have difficulties with managing their anxiety, and often their anxiety prevents them from living their lives as they would wish.

So, how do we ensure that we provide the optimum opportunities for unlocking and fulfilling potential, when we are faced with so many barriers?

Qualifications are fantastic. They are the currency for adult life that buys choice. But they should never be the only indicator of success. Eight GCSEs are not terribly useful if you are unable to leave your house due to your persistent and crippling levels of anxiety, or if you are totally unable to communicate with people that you don't already know. And as we all know, you can't learn if your head is full of worries.

At Limpsfield Grange we work on the broad areas of achievement, communication independence and wellbeing to measure success. We identify the gaps that each young person has, and design a tailored package to meet their needs. Can this young person function independently? Can they live safely? Can they communicate effectively with others? Can they manage change or uncertainty? Can they regulate their emotions effectively? Can they identify what keeps them emotionally, mentally and physically well? If the answer to any of these questions is "no" then we have to do something about it.

How we address the gaps is dependent on the young person, their needs and circumstances.

One bright ex-student found other people hard to understand, had anxiety levels off the scale and social vulnerabilities. She was a young carer; her mum had mental health difficulties and was unable to leave her house. But our student wanted to go to college so she could work with animals. In addition to meeting her wide ranging academic needs, we also worked with her to develop her independence skills in her home locality (practicing accessing bus routes, how to get to local amenities, how to book a doctor's appointment). We offered a short course of Cognitive Behavioural Therapy to help her manage her intrusive anxious thoughts, and worked with the NSPCC to help her to keep herself safe. Without these additional areas of support she would have left school with a raft of qualifications, but would have been unable to access a post 16 placement successfully. Qualifications on their own would not have been enough.

As educators we have a duty to enable the next generation to develop the right skills, tools and knowledge to thrive. I want the next generation of girls with special needs and disabilities to take their place in a world that respects and values them. I want these girls to live the life that they choose, and not live a life that is chosen for them. I want them to be proud of who they are, confident in knowing that they can make a contribution to society. I want them to be brave, because as Helen Keller said "life is either a great adventure or nothing."

Sarah Wild, Headteacher – Limpsfield Grange School

Sarah is the Headteacher of Limpsfield Grange School in Surrey, a state-funded residential special school for girls with communication and interaction difficulties including autism. She is interested in how autism impacts on, and manifests in girls and women, and in raising awareness of how autistic girls and boys present differently. This is the reason why we at Limpsfield Grange made "Girls with Autism," an ITV documentary which was aired in July 2015. Our students have also written two novels "M is for Autism" and "M in the Middle" with author Vicky Martin about their experiences of being autistic teenage girls.

Sarah is very interested in promoting and sustaining positive emotional wellbeing and mental health in young people with special needs in education settings.

@Head_Limpsfield

Striving for excellence for all

Like a precisely timed, perfectly choreographed formula one pit stop, it takes everyone to work in unison, at their optimum ability, to ensure the best possible outcomes for vulnerable children, irrespective of their starting points or their background. It takes an 'every second counts culture'. Each person to know and 'feel' their role and the absolute importance of it; where everyone is striving to be a little better than they were the day before; where they are gladly held to account and where everyone can succeed.

School culture does not happen by chance or by mistake. It is tenderly nurtured, honed and developed so that no matter what or who is being scrutinised the message remains unmistakable; we can succeed, we can excel and we can be great.

In such a culture, where all stakeholders are seen as learners, the goal is to consciously create an ethos where staff are encouraged to really know their children. They must take risks, reflect on their skills, create 'learning laboratories' in their rooms to share their learning; where no person, adult or child, is left behind or hidden. It is in this environment that rigorous accountability sits very much at the centre. It is the energy of adults that will drive school improvement and the children's successes so they need to be the right people. They, together with the leadership of the school, need to have a compelling moral purpose.

Absolute clarity about accountability is a must. It is this that will generate a commitment to dialogue and professional reflection. It must be partnered with organisational investment. Without clarity, accountability can quickly become the proverbial stick. For example, from the day she comes for her interview, the newly employed learning support assistant must know what the expectations of the school are. That they will have to create learning profiles and store evidence of the daily impact that they have with the children they work with. That they must be a role model in every respect; in their dress, their speech, their interactions. That they will have to 'read' the data and adapt interventions to suit the rapidly changing needs of the children. That they will have to be flexible to ensure that resources (including themselves) are targeted to meet pupil and staff needs. They will need to know the children inside out; their likes, dislikes, their backgrounds, their challenges.

They need to know that from day one, they are employed to make a difference. They need to understand the intrinsic hard work ahead; later they will share the joys of seeing the 'pupil statistically not expected to achieve' excel, and know that they played a part in that.

No one forgets a great teacher, and nor should they. A great teacher is, in the words of Sir John Jones, 'a magic-weaver; who can make a profound difference to the pupils they reach'. There can be no argument against this, but what about those less competent teachers who don't always reach the children they are trying to make a difference to? Those teachers who with the right support and accountability structures in place could have significant impact on more vulnerable and disadvantaged pupils where the need is greatest. A school's 'magic' must, therefore, lie in its honesty and integrity. It must ensure that all teachers and staff understand their moral accountability for the quality of teaching and its impact on individual pupils. Where there is a strong professional community that focuses on pedagogy and improvement. Robust evidence-based appraisal systems, on-going incisive coaching, rigorous and regular individual pupil data-led progress meetings. High quality training and targeted partnership teaching, coupled with open and honest feedback which ensures the consistency of high and quality teaching, need to be in place. Where the quality of teaching does fall below the required standard, a compelling moral purpose ensures that the capability procedure is rarely needed.

Positive beliefs and high expectations of adults and pupils alike may well be the most important factor in ensuring that vulnerable pupils achieve. Not only does it establish a culture of success, it draws upon a limitless resource and ensures that no pupil is left behind. This is not a government directive, nor fuelled by budget, it simply creates a 'language' for the school that all staff speak. Staff may not always have immediate answers to how to help a vulnerable individual achieve. But they will know the right questions to ask within an environment that fosters a shared approach to finding an answer.

Amanda Jennings, Headteacher – Ray Lodge Primary School

Amanda Jennings is headteacher of Ray Lodge Primary in Redbridge. She has been a headteacher for 12 years; and has enjoyed the challenge of leading two large primary schools. Ray Lodge Primary was awarded Outstanding status by Ofsted in September 2016.

A blank canvas:
releasing the imagination for all

Opening a school is like starting a work of art; the canvas is blank but we know which colours are possible and which brush strokes will be best. Leading a school, whether new or established, is as much about the vision and ethos as it is about developing systems and considering the practicalities, vision and ethos are the route map and spirit that guide the way, the decision to paint something beautiful. Without these there are only buildings and practicalities.

In September 2015, the University of Cambridge Primary School opened to a new community that was itself brand new, awaiting the arrival of 3500 new people to its vicinity. We did not know who our first intake were, what their learning needs would be or what their experiences of learning had been in the past. But our blank canvas was ready to be painted, supported by a clear vision and ethos and informed by research which meant we had a democratic and inclusive response to the question: what is the purpose of education?

Choosing the palette

Before we opened, we spent time reviewing literature about schooling and education; it was our preparing of the artist's palette. As with the Cambridge Primary Review (Alexander, 2010[11]) and Creating Learning without Limits (Swann, Peacock, Hart and Drummond, 2012[12]), we wanted our school vision to be based on empirical research with a democratic notion of education at its core. We wanted an educational experience that was about developing a 'shared, hopeful vision that pays attention to the diversity of perspectives in the human community' (Novak et al., 2014: p.5[13]) We wanted to challenge traditional notions of children's 'ability' as fixed to versions of 'transformability'. The idea was to develop a school community of people 'living educationally' (ibid. p.4); reflective, aspirational and actively engaged educators; and equally, children who were central to the principles and were co-constructors of their educational experience.

Our vision emanated from educational theorists who attempted to answer questions about the purpose of a democratic education. It grew organically from discussions, presentations and related to research. Maxine Greene's work especially resonated, bringing to light the educators' responsibility to find ways to 're-position perspectives' through an active engagement with 'open-space-making'.

---

11 Alexander, R.J. (ed) (2010) Children, their World, their Education: final report and recommendations of the Cambridge Primary Review. Oxon: Routledge.
12 Swann, M., Peacock, A., Hart, S., Drummond, M.J. (2012) Creating Learning without Limits. Maidenhead: McGraw-Hill International.
13 Novak, J., Armstrong, D., Browne, B. (2014) Leading for Educational Lives: inviting and sustaining imaginative acts of hope in a connected world, The Netherlands: SensePublishers

Painting the scene

To ensure that our new staff team, parents and children understood our purpose and vision, we needed to find multiple ways to articulate the learning culture we were intending to create. The vision started in the minds of a few people but it had to belong to everyone. Our aims were founded on three prinicples: **ambition, innovation** and **inclusion.**

- **Ambition** – everyone will be encouraged and enabled to achieve and attain highly.

- **Innovation** – the learning community will benefit from belonging to a research and teacher education community both within the school itself and as part of wider University and school partnerships.

- **Inclusion** – diversity will be welcomed in a caring environment where everybody will be valued.

Essentially, within a democratic environment, we wanted to teach children that learning is not a competition. Instead we wanted to inspire everyone to strive and learn from mistakes. We intended to foster our three principles of ambition, innovation and inclusion through a culture in which empathy, respect, trust, courage and gratitude were explicitly and implicitly taught. We wanted every voice to be valued and everyone empowered to be the best that he or she could be. Our view of democracy translated into the importance of collaboration, so that together everyone achieved more.

Beneath these principles, we developed five virtues or values that would guide our policies and approach to teaching and learning, behaviour management and various other practical matters. We considered these values to be vital to ensuring limitless possibilities to become a truth for our children and teachers. Within a culture of developing ideas, we identified the following values:

1. **Empathy:** listening carefully to others, learning together for the benefit of all.

2. **Respect**: treating everyone with dignity.

3. **Trust**: building relationships with a shared vision.

4. **Courage**: developing resilience, determination and releasing the imagination to develop possibility-thinking attitudes.

5. **Gratitude**: acknowledging one another with good manners, with thoughtfulness and consideration for each member of our community and the contribution they make.

And central to all this was our commitment to listening to children, encouraging dialogue and debate and finding opportunity for every voice to be heard.

Framing the painting

The children at our school know that learning is difficult. We tell them this all the time. We celebrate errors and the effort to find solutions. Children do not say, 'I can't do it' unless they add the word 'yet'. There is a growing culture of ideas so that all children, the vulnerable and the confident, can share without being laughed at. We do not give stickers or physical rewards because we want to focus on the value of successful learning. Instead, we talk to children about how they feel when they have achieved something through deliberate practice. We model new possibilities when they have struggled and we spend time talking with them to find better solutions. We believe that as well as the strategies and techniques to include the vulnerable children described in this book, a key focus must be on a wider school culture that expects the very best for all children. This is through a defining vision and ethos in which every child and teacher can share ideas, be acknowledged and be heard.

James Biddulph, Headteacher – University of Cambridge Primary School

James Biddulph is the first headteacher of the University of Cambridge Primary School. Prior to this, he opened a Hindu school and was Deputy in two schools. In 2003 he was awarded Outstanding New Teacher of the Year for London. He is currently completing his PhD on creative learning in ethnic minority home contexts.

@UniCamPrimSch

Recognising the strengths within 'Disadvantaged' communities

The term 'Disadvantaged' applies to nearly all our families. But again and again, members of our communities have created their own solutions about how to meet their own needs. There are many levels of networking and support going on. We host Arabic and Turkish classes. Churches and community groups use the school to celebrate their religious events. Our coffee mornings, curriculum and other events for families are always well attended. We work closely with REACT, a local community group whose members give voice to the concerns of the community, highlighting the frustrations faced by people who, at times, feel forgotten by service providers. So we have a level of community cohesion which works together whilst navigating the challenges presented by poverty.

Many new families have no access to public funds. We have children and families from fifty-six different countries. Some have had a calm move to this country and some, sadly, have had extremely traumatic experiences. One of our foci is creating a safe and harmonious school environment where fears and anxieties are reduced, through a strong pastoral system.

Continuously, children join us in all year groups with no experience of speaking English. This comes with different challenges based on the age of the child.

Early Years and Key Stage 1 children will have, if they stay with us, time to reach stage three with confidence, with elements of stage four (on a five stage EAL criteria.) Starting in Key Stage 2 (at any point in years 3, 4, 5 or 6) presents a shorter time to develop English to access the complexity of the curriculum. Our 'Beginners in English' Group which takes place for an hour and a quarter on four afternoons a week, helps to accelerate children's access to both spoken and written English. We also have a 'Breakthrough to Literacy', with a focus on Oracy, which gives children some security in being able to speak and write in a new language, within a nurturing environment. The immersion and the focused session approaches work well, giving children time in class and offering them a break from the pressure of listening in a language that they don't yet speak.

Through the school's Pastoral team and Children's Centre, we harness the support of community partners in bringing services which include Health (pre and post birth), Job Centre+ Mental Health Services and many others. This enables families to make best use of these services locally. It takes time and patience for our new families to learn to trust that we are interested in their wellbeing, rather than wanting to intervene in their 'business' or have their children taken away from them. Once we have secured their trust, we see adults blossom in their new community; which then impacts on their children. Our Pastoral team provide a safe haven for families who are distressed and ensure that they access the relevant services, often accompanying a parent to appointments to give them support in expressing their needs and concerns, sourcing funds for clothing and household items, and small scale renovation. Our Pastoral Officer is a food bank ambassador and is a source of strength in enabling our neediest families in accessing food and other resources.

Education is the route out of poverty, to ensure each child receives the high quality learning opportunities we would want for our own children. This means that those who choose to work in our community need to be committed to walking those extra miles. Whilst most parents and carers who can support their children's educational development do so, some, due to a host of experiences, and who do want the best for their children just do not have the academic learning to enable them to help sufficiently. They can, however support their childrens high expectations. Expect their children to try their best at school and complete their homework. We would never label parents and very few teachers, I would suggest, have walked in their shoes.

As a school we simply need to take on the extra responsibilities of ensuring that schooling and social care are tightly linked, through identifying the possible needs of our most vulnerable children and putting systems in place to help them break the cycle of familial and community deprivation.

We must also ensure that the success of all children is our focus which will change the life chances of not only themselves but also their future families.

The recently published Counting the Cost of Poverty, by The Rowntree Foundation[14] suggests that the average cost of poverty in the UK is around £78 billion. Within that figure the 'identifiable knock-on effects of child poverty cost £6 billion and the knock-on effects of adult poverty cost at least £2.7 billion'.

The school and community live with these 'knock-on effects' daily.

There are a range of strategies we use to support most vulnerable pupils. Our Nurture Group is a small group of the most vulnerable children, with social, emotional and behavioural development needs. They have usually experienced significant trauma. The Nurture Group is run by a teacher and a teaching assistant. Children are assessed against criteria based on the Boxall Profile and the outcomes of this diagnostic provide a starting point for intervention support. The programme focuses on the needs of six and seven year olds, with some ongoing support in Key Stage 2. Children can spend up to four terms in the Nurture Group, with some time each day in their home classes.

This level of support is vital for some of the neediest of children and enables them to develop trust and self-worth.

A small number of children take part in our 'Tiger Team' pre-school programme where activities, run by trained Teaching Assistants, support children in developing their gross and fine motor skills, and core strength and balance. Breakfast Club is well attended and the breakfast materials are funded. Our early

---

14 See www.jrf.org.uk/report/counting-cost-uk-poverty

morning programmes, which include additional reading writing/grammar and maths support for small numbers, also provide breakfast for all who attend.

As proposed by the All Party Parliamentary Group on Children's Centres (July 2016) the "Family Hubs" should result in Children's Centres becoming "The **'go to'** place for any parents to access services or information about all family-related matters. These might include birth registration, antenatal and postnatal services, employment and debt advice, substance misuse services, relationship and parenting support, local activities for families and support for families separating. This level of aftercare support is vital to ensure that we, in some measure, break the cycle of familial challenges for some of our children. What the example below demonstrates is that successful learning for some children is nothing short of a miracle when we consider their home/community circumstances.

> A single mum, whose partner was in prison. Initially she had challenges with drugs and she fought for a long time to change some of her habits. She was signposted to our outreach team which resulted in her being evicted. She was really concerned about how other parents, and staff, might perceive her and was reluctant to engage with our team. Her fear was that Social Services would take her children. It took over a year of gentle support and encouragement for her to feel safe, initially much of her time with us being focused around one member of staff. She needed time to understand and appreciate that we were not there to judge her and very gradually she engaged. She also felt more comfortable with the understanding that her information would be shared on a 'need to know basis' with other agencies. A member of the team went to dental appointments with her as she had not visited the dentist since she was a little girl. She accessed support from Social Services, Health, Solace, Compass, counselling service, volunteer training agency. She also began to take an active part in Stay and Play sessions and then started volunteering. She has also started college. She is now very much in charge of her own wellbeing and says she is able to say 'no' when being encouraged to go back to her 'old' life. Her children are much more settled in school.

It is the hidden side of school life and offers an insight into the importance of working with the adults to enable the children to have better life chances.

We need to offer support in helping some of our families to break the cycle that has become a survival strategy for most of their lives.

Our community needs are complex. With the school taking its role as the hub of the community extremely seriously, some of the obstacles can be removed and opportunities taken up, even where poverty seems so deeply entrenched.

Marva Rollins OBE, Headteacher – Raynham Primary School

Marva Rollins OBE has used her 22 years as a Headteacher to work hard to give children and families the opportunities to excel and overcome the barriers presented by low socioeconomic conditions. She has also trained, coached and mentored future education leaders. She is a legacy builder.

@head182ray

Training fleas: Why we should stop making excuses for our disadvantaged pupils

Fleas are amazing creatures, they can jump 100 times their own height, which is the equivalent of a 6ft human leaping a 30 storey building, but if you put them in a jar with a lid, within three days of jumping against this imposed ceiling this feat will no longer be achievable. Even when the lid is removed, the fleas will have learnt to jump no higher than where the lid was placed. What is even more amazing is that their offspring will also be able to jump no higher, having followed the example of their parents.

Are we unconsciously creating the same effect in our schools, particularly for those labelled 'disadvantaged?'

We need to stop making excuses for why our pupils can't achieve. The only ceiling all children have is the one that we place on them.

The first of 7 building blocks to tackling disadvantage highlighted in 'what successful schools are doing'[15] is ensuring that schools have an ethos of achievement for all, but how is this achieved?

- **Stop making excuses.** All staff and stakeholders need to buy into the fact that all children can achieve. That means we don't make excuses for SEN children, or children who have difficult home lives. This needs to be clear in staff performance management meetings. Our job as professionals is not to say why they 'won't make it' but instead what we can do to get them there.

- **Don't make assumptions.** Disadvantaged is not a group it's a label. We need to stop trying to find the magic bullet, it doesn't exist. Instead we need to work out what the 'disadvantage' for each individual child in our schools is (and yes, some children may have several). We know that the research tells us that 'disadvantaged pupils have less support at home' but we need to be careful about assuming that this is true of all of our disadvantaged pupils. We need to not take research as the identification of a barrier that affects all, but instead as a starting point. Use it to work out if this is truly applicable to your school and to which pupils in particular. A blanket approach will end up targeting pupils who may have a different need entirely. Not all 'disadvantaged' pupils need a homework club or music lessons. The only way you can find this out is by talking to pupils, their families and the staff who work with the pupils on a daily basis.

- **Know your data.** Looking at 'disadvantaged' as a collective is not enough, we need to unpick the different groups that sit within this to ensure our provision is right for all. How do SEN 'disadvantaged' pupils progress

15 www.gov.uk/government/uploads/system/uploads/attachment_data/file/473974/DFE-RR411_
Supporting_the_attainment_of_disadvantaged_pupils.pdf

compared to other SEN children in your school? What about 'disadvantaged' white boys? More importantly what about higher achieving disadvantaged pupils (or those that could be high achieving if we stopped talking about them as 'on track')?

- **Think strategically.** Enrichment and inclusion are important parts of any pupil premium budget, but we must remember that our biggest focus when deciding how to spend the pupil premium is how to have the biggest impact on learning outcomes. The most significant way to do this is ensuring that all pupils have access to good/outstanding teaching. Therefore this should be a primary focus in every school. Having multiple interventions running for 'disadvantaged' children simply highlights that a school has not yet tackled the barriers its children are facing. Instead of intervention we need to be better at anticipating the barriers and planning for the provision that will counteract these. A focus on identification instead of intervention will not only mean that we can get to the root causes quicker, but it will also be a lot more cost effective.

- **Solve the problem.** As educators we spend everyday trying to deliver difficult concepts to pupils and when they are unable to grasp something, we think of another way to deliver it so that they can achieve. We don't teach a child addition in a week and if they don't get it give up. It's the same with our 'pupil premium strategy'. Our first solution may not be the one that makes a difference, we may have to tweak delivery or change it entirely, but we should be proud of the journey that leads us towards improvement. We need to follow the advice that we so frequently give our pupils that we learn best from our mistakes.

- **Remember what's good for one should be good for all.** Recent guidance from the NAHT on website compliance states that 'schools should be able to discuss how they have used the pupil premium to benefit all pupils' which makes sense really. If we are focused on improving outcomes for all then outcomes for 'disadvantaged' pupils will also improve. Remember we're not competing with an 'in school gap' but instead we're focused on closing the gap against 'national other'. The most successful strategies are the ones that ensure that all pupils achieve in the classroom, for example getting teachers to identify learning barriers for all children in their class, or teachers mentoring each other to improve their practice.

- **Be teachers and learners not experts.** We need to get better at sharing. So many schools feel that they haven't 'cracked' disadvantaged yet, but every school will have experienced some successes. Whether it's successful transition arrangements or increased progress in a particular subject or year group, everyone has something to shout about. So don't keep quiet just because the achievement feels too small to celebrate. We all need to learn from each other instead of waiting for an expert to appear. We are each other's best solution in improving outcomes for disadvantaged learners. We just need to find the right forums to share and listen.

Kate Masters, Lead Practitioner – Vulnerable Learners – Borough of Poole

Kate Masters is an experienced teacher and senior leader, employed by the Borough of Poole to raise standards for disadvantaged pupils. She works with Primary and Secondary schools to identify how they can improve their provision and supports them in implementing this. She also runs 'Pupil Premium Network' events to share best practice.

No Excuses

The accountability culture in British education for the last twenty years or more means that leaders can see students' backgrounds as challenges rather than opportunities. I certainly did and have had to reflect on why I made excuses for poor student outcomes based on demographic factors and anecdotal reasons. Leaders of any organisation are responsible for a multitude of tasks; establishing and articulating the core purpose and strategic direction are arguably the most essential for the longevity and success of the organisation.[16]

As school leaders, we are fully aware of the need to promote our own school's vision and values and are regularly rewarded when we see first-hand the development of our students into adults ready to face the challenges that lie ahead. We charge ourselves with the responsibility that all students can fulfil their undoubted potential. We are, however, required to absorb and align ourselves with external change which is all too often decided without our involvement.

The introduction of the Pupil Premium in April 2011 gave school leaders an opportunity to use the fund to address the gap in disadvantaged students' attainment which prevails throughout their school career[17]. Many schools, along with my own, floundered in part because it took time to understand which factors have the greatest impact on students' outcomes and their future expectations.

As headteacher, I needed a paradigm shift in my perspective about how students' backgrounds affected their examination outcomes. I needed to see the barriers as an opportunity for school leaders and staff to make a difference in a profound way rather than as obstacles to justify underachievement.

After a Section 8 Ofsted inspection in May 2015, school leaders at Ruislip High School, with the support and challenge of school governors, established a comprehensive strategic action plan. A number of valuable lessons have been learnt and are summarised as follows:

Effective teachers: Partly based on the Sutton Trust research (2011)[18], our disadvantaged students are now given teachers who can make the biggest difference, providing students with the confidence that they can succeed. This is in complete contrast to previous years when lower achieving GCSE classes, that had a high proportion of disadvantaged students, were taught by agency teachers. The GCSE results this summer, in particular English, showed the impact of this approach.

Whole-school approach: We have established a coordinated approach to intervention which means a clear set of core beliefs have been shared with all staff.

---

16 Pendeleton, D. & Furnham, A. (2012). Leadership: All You Need to Know. London: Palgrave Macmillan
17 Ofsted (2013). Unseen children: access and achievement 20 years on.
18 Sutton Trust (2011). Improving the impact of teachers on pupil achievement in the UK – interim findings.

The provision for support and intervention is now coordinated by a senior leader, and classroom teachers are made to feel accountable through a referral system and setting work for tutors to do with their students on a one-to-one basis.

Key Stage 3 focus: We concentrate our efforts on Key Stage 3 (which has the highest proportion of disadvantaged students), ensuring that our lower attaining students have ongoing support with literacy and numeracy. Based on our own evidence for the past two years, the school is likely to establish a nurture class at Key Stage 3 in September 2017, rather than continue with intervention during lessons; this will mean students being withdrawn from some foundation subjects to allow for intensive literacy and numeracy development. This is a reflection of another core belief that our approach is flexible and therefore we can adapt to the needs of different cohorts based on the evaluation of evidence.

Methodology to evaluate initiatives and interventions: There is now a clear format for how schemes and initiatives are reviewed. Impact evaluation reports are reviewed termly by governors and used to write the evaluation of Pupil Premium spending. Comparative data is an essential part of the evaluation methodology in terms of comparison of progress between students involved in the intervention with other students in their cohort as well as sub-group analysis. In the majority of cases, disadvantaged students make the least amount of progress compared to other students involved in the intervention.

Parental engagement: I fully endorse the position espoused by research into students' achievement that schools have a 20% influence compared with personal and social factors attributing for 80%. This evidence allows school leaders to consider their schools' demographics and consider how parents can be supported to try to be involved in their child's education.[19]

Based on this year's review, disadvantaged students are now categorised into three groups: non-vulnerable, vulnerable and hard-to-reach. Our two part-time, family-liaison officers work primarily with the last group. They have been trained in a parenting programme which allows them to provide support and advice for parents based on the principles of the scheme. Their mantra is that each family is a 'book' and their involvement is to help support and nurture a 'different chapter'. They have made a significant difference to a number of families and students' outcomes based on their ability to change some of the personal and social factors that are a barrier to students' education.

With the introduction of the Year 7 catch-up fund, Ruislip High introduced an initiative called Core Kick Start (CKS). This involves families of Year 6 students joining the school to attend after-school lessons with their parents from June until October in English and/or mathematics. It is a scheme that has been evaluated in terms of student outcomes as well as parental attitudinal data. CKS is in its fourth

---

19 Pont, B., Nusche, D., & Moorman, H. (2008). Improving School Leadership. Vol 1: Policy and Practice. Paris: OECD

year and the evaluation process has allowed a number of modifications which has improved the scheme each year.

Personalised approach: Assistant Heads of Year for each year group have been appointed with one year contracts. These contracts are only renewed if their impact on disadvantaged pupils is clear. One of their primary targets is to improve the attendance of disadvantaged students. The impact of their hard work and a number of their initiatives during 2016-2017, for example support for students when they are absent, led to an increase in disadvantaged students' attendance by 1.46%; this narrowed the gap with other students by 1.11%. There have been termly meetings with the senior leadership link and Head of Year; this allowed for each student to be discussed individually and the impact of actions to be reviewed. Even with this personalised approach, raising the number of disadvantaged students who participate in residential trips continues to be a target. We have also introduced link-governors in the role as advocates for our most able students at Key Stage 4. This decision is supported by research evidence into how students' expectations change as they get older. Between the ages of 14 and 16, students from low-income families are more likely to change their expectation about a previous ambition to go to university. The scheme now involves three governors working with three disadvantaged students who have the potential to progress to higher education; this will be reviewed at the end of the year.[20]

Key recommendations

School leaders and governors should ensure that:

- the progress of disadvantaged students is a whole-school priority, with clearly defined roles and responsibilities including link governors;

- disadvantaged students have the most effective teachers;

- parent engagement is established and maintained through a number of key staff;

- a personalised approach is used and disadvantaged students are separated into meaningful categories which allows leaders to prioritise and target specific resources;

- there is an effective methodology with a clear plan to measure the impact of interventions which includes comparative data;

- there are key individuals, eg. governors or outside mentors, who can support disadvantaged students with their future expectations.

To conclude, we need to be conscious that whilst accountability measures change with different agendas by politicians and inspectors, it is essential that we do

20 Chowdrey, H., Crawford, C., & Goodman, A. (2009). Drivers and Barriers to Educational Success: Evidence from the Longitudinal Study of Young People in England. London: Institute for Fiscal Studies/DCSF

not lose sight of our values and core purpose, and even change them because of external pressures. The potential of every child is by its very nature unquantifiable. School leaders must have the moral imperative that students' backgrounds should never be a reason to lower our expectations of their future capabilities.[21]

Martina Lecky, Headteacher – Ruislip High School

Dr Martina Lecky was appointed Headteacher of Ruislip High School (RHS) in September 2011. Her Doctorate in Education, awarded by King's College London, was on teachers' professional development in the context of the Cognitive Acceleration through Science Education (CASE) progress. She is a member of the Let's Think Council and also one of the Let's Think Forum's trustees.

Following the RHS's GCSE results in 2014, she, along with senior leaders and governors, implemented a strategic action plan to improve disadvantaged students' attainment; this has led to significant improvements, removing the English and mathematics GCSE attainment gap between RHS's disadvantaged students and 'other' students nationally.

21 Tomsett, J. (2015). *This Much I Know About Love Over Fear ...: Creating a Culture for Truly Great Teaching.* Carmarthen: Crown House Publishing.

PRACTICAL STRATEGIES

The purpose of this book is to help improve outcomes for vulnerable learners. This section is all about 'how to'. It aims to provide solutions for challenges that schools can begin to implement tomorrow.

Kate Atkins, Headteacher, Rosendale Primary School | Tackling the Language Gap | Practical, evidence based strategies to tackle language poverty, one of the key causes of educational disadvantage.

Loic Menezies and Eleanor Bernardes, LKMco |Youth Work and Schools: A untapped opportunity for Partnership? | How schools can effectively work with youth organisations to support vulnerable learners.

James Hollinsley, Headteacher, Longwood Primary Academy | A pathway for tackling the Unknown | A proactive approach to better mental health and emotional wellbeing in primary schools.

Scott Palmer, Deputy Headteacher, Rosendale Primary School | More Effective use of TAs | The practical application of the growing evidence base on Teaching Assistants.

Bridget Clay, Network Programme Manager, Teacher Development Trust | Developing Teachers to enable great learning for vulnerable pupils | The importance of teaching for vulnerable learners is undisputed: How can we ensure that professional development can have maximum impact on pupils.

Liz Bramley, Headteacher, Oakdene Primary School | It takes a village to raise a child | Best practice in supporting learners post adoption.

Richard Kieran, Headteacher, Woodrow First School | Waiting for the right time to speak; knowing you'll be heard | The importance of oracy for disadvantaged learners.

Michelle Haywood, SEN and Inclusion Manager, EnTrust | Cracks in the Pavement: Disadvantaged Learners and University | Personal reflections and practical solutions for schools to support disadvantaged pupils into university.

Jon Richards, Head of Education, Unison | How Support Staff can improve outcomes for vulnerable learners | What the evidence says, and a case study about some of the most vulnerable pupils in our schools.

Rachel Rossiter, SENCO, The Bury Trust | Supporting Struggling Readers at KS3 | Practical solutions to help tackle poor literacy, and to better understand the causes of poor literacy.

Sameena Choudry on Black, Asian and Minority Ethnic Achievement | How to effectively support pupils in our increasingly diverse schools.

Stuart Lock, Headteacher, Cottingham Village College | Access to the community of educated citizens | How a knowledge-rich curriculum opens up opportunity to participate in and improve society and community.

Rob Webster, Researcher – Centre for Inclusive Education, UCL Institute of Education | Relocation Relocation Relocation: Managing school transfer for high mobility families | Practical strategies to minimize the impact of mobility on pupil outcomes and emotional wellbeing.

Stephen Betts, CEO - Learn Sheffield | Young carers | Improving provision and outcomes for pupils who care for others.

Every year, a majority of children entering the Early Years', lack basic age-appropriate numeracy, speech and language and self-help regulation skills. For the strongest possible outcomes and the best foundation for secondary school is made possible through rigid and relentless focus upon their learning.

Clear targets with high expectations are a necessary starting point. The Governing Body and Leadership Team work to the central goal that each child in the school, without exception, will make better than expected progress, across each Key Stage and throughout their time in St. Joseph's. This aim is to ensure that every pupil makes the necessary progress to attain well. Crafting a 'personalised learning journey' for each child is a necessary step to deliver this target. In turn, this requires all staff and leaders to see children beyond any limiting labels. We believe in high expectations for every child, without exception.

The school's approach grows from a successful combination of a focus upon the needs of each individual child. Alongside this, the creation and nurturing of school as an environment where everyday practice delivers appropriate challenge, support and builds confidence in every child. A child's every experience in school, every lesson, every play-time, every extra-curricular activity or school trip must act in support of these goals.

Helen Tyler, St Joseph's Catholic Primary School, Camden

Tackling the Language Gap

"Simply by making noises with our mouths, we can reliably cause precise new combinations of ideas to arise in each other's minds. The ability comes so naturally that we are apt to forget what a miracle it is," said Stephen Pinker in his book '*The Language Instinct*' perfectly describing the extraordinary function of language.

Many teachers, senior leaders and researchers are more and more convinced that educational disadvantage stems from language poor environments, from the lack of access to vocabulary and a lack of ability to play with language. Children from language poor environments do not develop the skills to create ideas in each other's minds. As Pie Corbett, headteacher, former Ofsted inspector and well known promoter of language in classrooms, offers this simple explanation "You cannot write it if you cannot say it; you cannot say it if you haven't heard it."

There are statistics to support our convictions. A study in 2008 (Atlantic, Boston Globe, LENA Natural Language Study) found that a child from a professional family hears 2,153 words per hour, whilst a child from a family on welfare hears 616 words per hour. And data from our schools shows that children from 'disadvantaged' backgrounds (measured by eligibility for free school meals) perform much worse than other children at the end of each key stage. And this gap widens as the children get older.

I am going to argue that educational establishments have to make language learning and development their key priority. That all settings should self-audit to see how much language is being used in their classrooms, by who and of what quality.

What should we be looking for? Let's first think about those professional households belting out over 2,000 words an hour. We know that one of the key things at this early stage of language learning is that adults are talking. They are talking to each other and children are hearing high level conversations with all the nuances and responses and emotion that goes with that. These parents are also talking to their children. They use words to engage the children in the world around them, explaining and making sense of things. Take for example a trip to a supermarket or travelling on a bus. We have all been in these situations and seen toddlers get bored and shout or cry or use other attention seeking behaviours. And we have seen parents using language to alleviate the boredom and improve the quality of the experience by involving the children. This often involves a running commentary for example describing what is outside the bus window or what needs to be bought from each aisle and why. Parents also involve children in making choices "Daddy likes this one, Mummy likes that one. Which one do you think we should have? You choose" and introduce higher order questioning "Why do you think that dog is wagging his tail so hard?"

These are some of the language experiences that some children have access to and that we must try and replicate in our Early Years settings. I like to hear adults talking to each other in Early Years, sharing experiences, asking for advice, making each other laugh. These are all wonderful language models for children to hear. I also want adults to provide a language model through a 'running commentary' for play activities.

Last summer, I spent a wonderful hour playing with a group of toddlers and some water play. We had a canal with gates in it which when closed stopped the flow of water down the canal. When enough water had built up behind the gates, we opened the gates and the flow of water carried the toy boats down the canal and into tray at the bottom. We then closed the gate, brought the boats back up and started the process all over again.

Children want to repeat activities over and over again and they are right to do so as the repetition builds the neural pathways they will need so the action becomes easier and easier. The same is true of language. Initially the children had no words to describe what was happening, so I provided a repeated commentary on what was happening and tried to use the same words every time I said it. The commentary was timed to fit the actions. By the end of the session, all the children could use the new language to describe the activity, predict what would happen and to instruct others who came to join in. "Open gate" shouted one little boy to me who was waiting by the water tray for the boats to appear. "Boat floating?" asked another when I asked him what would happen if I opened the gate. Early Years Professionals understand that they are creating a language rich experience and that the play based classrooms provide so many opportunities for children to talk. To talk to adults and to talk to their peers.

Start by auditing your Early Years provision. Find out how much talk is happening. If you have the capacity, complete a simple tally chart over the course of a day to see how much adults are talking and what kind of talking it is. Is it running commentary, instructions, questions (if so how many elicit a response), storytelling, conversation with other adults, talking to parents? Also make sure that staff are spending more time talking with children than observing them.

One of the problems with baseline assessment and the foundation stage profile is that staff have felt the burden of providing evidence and are spending more teaching time gathering evidence rather than educating. Look at the quality of interactions and also the quantity. Make sure your staff are talking more with disadvantaged learners than others as they are the ones who need it more. They are also the children who tend to want to be outside engaging in physical play, so make sure that the staff have strategies to bring language to activities involving climbing or riding bikes. Make sure that the role play area is changed regularly so that it appeals to all children and make sure that staff spend time in this area modelling language structures. Find out if the planning includes key language structures that all staff know about and are modelling to children. It is also useful to ask staff about how they make use of spontaneous opportunities for talk such as finding a snail or talking about the puddles that have appeared in the playground.

These language rich environments can be (and must be) recreated throughout primary and secondary schools in order to support our vulnerable learners. If you walked round your school how much planned-for language teaching would you find? By this I don't mean 'talk to your partner' but activities that are structured and scaffolded to make sure that children use language correctly and understand it.

Regularly reviewing language development has made us focus on how children are using language in the classroom. Can they use key vocabulary? Can they have fun with language? Can they manipulate language? Can they generate questions as well as answers? Can they argue their case and persuade others? Over the years, as we have reviewed language in our classrooms, we have discovered the following things.

- When you set or stream, disadvantaged learners suffer from the lack of great peer to peer language support

- If you don't pre-teach vocabulary when reading, you leave many children unable to participate because they don't understand the content

- Engagement, language and enjoyment are all enhanced by hands on experiences

- Learning stories off by heart improves children's use of language

- Providing a 'running commentary' helps children access the language they need

- Children need support in order to be able to use specific language structures

- Disadvantaged learners do better in class discussions when they have had opportunities to practice the language

- Disadvantaged learners thrive when they have more conversations with their teachers

These discoveries have had an enormous impact on teaching and learning. It has changed the way classrooms are organised, for example, all our children sit in mixed achievement teams. It has sent us out to find how other schools improve outcomes for disadvantaged learners and as a result of our travels we have introduced reciprocal reading and talk for writing.

Every school is different with its own context. However, access to language is something that all schools need to provide in order to support disadvantaged learners. What would you find if you did a language audit in your school? And what steps would you take in order to improve language learning?

Kate Atkins, Headteacher – Rosendale Primary School

Kate Atkins is Headteacher of Rosendale Primary School an 'outstanding' three form entry school with three Children's Centre. Kate Atkins has been teaching in Lambeth for over 20 years. Although she has taught across the primary age range, her specialism and her passion is in Early Years.

@kateatkins33

Youth Work and Schools:
An untapped opportunity for partnership?

Schools and school-leaders up and down the country are currently struggling under the increasing pressure of accountability and intensive reform. Yet extra help could be available if stronger partnerships could be forged between schools and youth organisations.

Research by LKMco and the charity 'London Youth' shows that there are many roles schools play in supporting vulnerable learners which they do not feel well placed to provide. Some of these areas include facilitating access to support in periods of crisis, and providing opportunities to learn about sex and relationships. These are particularly crucial for vulnerable learners.

One response to these 'confidence deficits' could be to call for more teacher training and more curriculum time devoted to them. But schools and teachers cannot be experts at everything. Instead, the burden on teachers needs to be reduced whilst ramping up support for vulnerable learners. Working with the youth sector (including youth clubs, youth workers and the organisations that employ them), could help bring school workload under control whilst boosting support for those who need it most.

Closer collaboration between schools and youth work is not a new idea. In 1969 the Fairburn-Milson committee called for greater integration between schools and youth work. It even encouraged the creation of joint teacher – youth worker posts. Investment in youth services as a whole increased in the late 1990s under New Labour, but youth work increasingly came to be seen as a vehicle for addressing the needs of NEET young people (Not in Education Employment or Training).

Closer collaboration with schools remained elusive under Michael Gove, when a renewed focus on academic education further exacerbated the issue. This was not helped by the austerity measures that followed after the 2008 financial crisis. The concept of the 'Big Society' also played a role in reshaping the sector, with the community and voluntary sector increasingly expected to fill gaps left behind by shrinking local services. According to some, this approach constituted a threat to the sector's professionalism.

Despite the strains the youth sector has been placed under, LKMco and London Youth's research shows that school leaders already recognise the sector's complementary expertise. In particular, in providing opportunities for active citizenship and learning beyond the classroom. The potential benefits of further collaboration remain significant since youth workers' focus on pastoral and developmental priorities can help them develop specialist expertise to help support transition to work. Youth workers can also draw on more informal relationships with students that act as a strong foundation to support vulnerable learners lacking in home support. Drawing on an alternative or 'third' relationship (neither parent nor teacher) may also be particularly useful when young people are going through periods of transition, for example between school phases.

Unfortunately, a range of barriers currently stand in the way of closer collaboration. Some, such as lack of resources or adequate information, are logistical. Others run deeper with schools sometimes highlighting concerns about incompatible ways of working or revealing outdated negative images of youth clubs and youth workers. There is also a risk that where individual teachers or leaders are championing the approach, they are unable to embed it into whole school thinking.

Yet some schools have embraced closer partnership with youth services and are using these to widen the opportunities available to learners. Bishop Challoner Catholic Girls School in Tower Hamlets for example, works with the youth organisation "Reach Out" to provide mentoring and enrichment activities. These are specifically targeted at disadvantaged and vulnerable learners. The project puts particular emphasis on building bridges between evening or out-of-school activities and the classroom, ensuring that learning can be transferred between settings and reinforced.

Another partnership in Streatham, South London, sees older learners from Norbury Manor School working with younger peers who are at risk of under-achievement or who are facing other challenges. Structured sessions take place on a regular basis at the local youth club. The project has now been running for two years and is delivering strong outcomes, both for the younger group and the older facilitators.

In another example of an innovative partnership, the charity ThinkForward (which is funded by Impetus PEF), places "progression coaches" in schools to work with pupils at risk of becoming NEET.

Tellingly, the organisation intentionally avoids the language of 'youth-work' to bypass misconceptions.

Skillfully implemented, a school and youth club partnership has the potential to widen opportunities and to make use of additional expertise and capacity. This is a valuable way of increasing support for vulnerable learners. It is important to plan how learning will be transferred between settings and to avoid dependence on single individuals within schools or youth organisations. Furthermore, in order to avoid clashes of approach, youth workers and schools should work together to agree goals and ways of working, tackling any differences of approach from the beginning. Finally, teachers and youth workers should explicitly recognise each other's skill-sets and acknowledge their mutual value when speaking to students so as to reinforce each other's work.

Rather than trying to do everything themselves, schools should work with youth organisations that have the time and expertise needed to provide the wraparound support many vulnerable learners need.

Loic Menzies, Director and Eleanor Bernardes, Associate – LKMco

Loic Menzies is Director of the education and youth 'think and action-tank' LKMco. He has also been a Tutor for Canterbury Christ Church University's Faculty of Education and is a trustee of The Kite Trust. He was previously Associate Senior Manager at St. George's R.C. School and a youth-worker before that.

@LKMco

Eleanor Bernardes is an Associate at LKMco with over ten years' experience in education. She has carried out extensive research in areas such as creative writing, SEND and careers education. She has worked with the International Baccalaureate Organisation and was awarded a distinction for her MA in Educational Leadership.

@Nor_edu

A Pathway for tackling the unknown

Poor mental health can harm our youngest members of society. The damage in later life can be life-limiting, life-threatening, and irreparable. It can lead to further generations experiencing the same. For those who are fortunate, help is found. For those less fortunate, they suffer dreadfully. Sometimes, the consequences are incomprehensible.

The facts

- 10% of children and young people (aged 5-16 years) have a clinically **diagnosable mental health problem**, yet 70% of these have **not had appropriate interventions** at an early age.[22]

- Over the last ten years the number of people being admitted to hospital because of **self-harm** has increased by 68%.[23]

- **Suicide** is the leading cause of death in young people (male and female) in their twenties and early thirties. **Suicide attempts** are up to 20 times more frequent than completed suicides.[24]

- 95% of **imprisoned young offenders** have a mental health disorder. Many of them are struggling with more than one disorder.[25]

- Alongside the detrimental price to the individual and their families, the **long-term cost to the UK economy** is £105 billion per year[26]. This is in *reaction* to what is already happening.

The Progress Approach

In March 2016, the DfE published its guidance document 'Mental Health and Behaviour in Schools' outlining schools' responsibility to promote pupils' mental health. At Longwood Primary Academy in Harlow we have developed an innovative whole school approach in fulfilling this responsibility. The PROGRESS model has proven effective in promoting pupils' social, emotional and mental health needs.

---

22 Mental Health Statistics: Children and Young People, Mental Health Foundation, (2016) www.mentalhealth.org.uk/statistics/mental-health-statistics-children-and-young-people

23 YoungMinds (2011) 100,000 children and young people could be hospitalised due to self-harm by 2020 warns YoungMinds. London: YoungMinds

24 Suicide Statistics, Befrienders Worldwide, (2016) www.befrienders.org/suicide-statistics

25 Office for National Statistics (1997): Psychiatric morbidity among young offenders in England and Wales. London: Office for National Statistics.

26 The Five Year Forward View for Mental Health, NHS England, (2016) www.england.nhs.uk/wp-content/uploads/2016/02/Mental-Health-Taskforce-FYFV-final.pdf

Provide a place to talk and feel protected
Raise the roof of resilience
Openly celebrate achievements
Grow and nurture the family unit
Rapid intervention and referral
E-safety to reduce risk
Strive to create a secure utopia
Stability and clarity in behaviour

Provide a place to talk and feel protected

- Use 'Time to Talk' with Place2Be. This is an additional service, outside of the 12 counselling sessions, and is an approach that can be used by all schools. Pupils fill in a form and put it in a post box. They can select an adult to talk to and name a friend they would like to join them.

- Genuinely listen to pupils when they come to you – what may seem a trivial matter could feel colossal to them. Follow up with them, so this way they know you care.

- Enhance pupil voice – Pupil Advocates, Class Advocates, School Improvement Officers, House Captains, School Council, voting stations, fortnightly votes and take on board their ideas for school events. Include those most vulnerable – develop their inner voice.

- Ensure whole staff awareness of those pupils who are vulnerable.

Raise the roof of resilience

- Know the limit of the most vulnerable pupils, then raise it inch-by-inch over time. Know when to change focus and not continue to avoid failure.

- Allow the pupils to reflect when they are in a place to do so after an incident. What happened? What shall we do next time?

- Focus on the cause – Be calm in the face of outbursts – maintain a supportive relationship.

- Develop trust over time and keep consistent.

- Develop an ethos of self-belief 'we cannot...yet', rather than 'we cannot.'

Openly celebrate achievements

- Some children want to be praised but do not like this in a large forum e.g. assemblies. A simple High Five and a smile can be just as powerful as being on stage. Showing work to a friend or significant adult works well for those who don't always lie attention.

- Develop a cluster of well planned 'praise' routes – brilliant book, house points, reward time, headteacher awards, class points, emails/phone calls home, activities. These are to be within the behavioural approach and all adults should be aware of these.

- Use art to increase the self-confidence and status of some vulnerable pupils – pieces commissioned onto acrylic – and include their work in an Art Exhibition to which families will be invited.

Grow and nurture the family unit

- Take time to know the parents and also the wider family. For example, it could be an older sibling who supports parents in making important decisions.

- Presentations and workshops – engage the most vulnerable families.

- Family Support Worker and Safeguarding Officer – both with an extended hours policy.

- Develop the parents' trust in the school, understand what barriers exist, and whether the school accentuates them. Knock down the barriers and let them see for themselves that things have changed.

- Focus on 'working together' – a two-way relationship rather than the school doing something to the family or individual.

Rapid intervention and referral

- Open dialogue regarding concerns, and the reasons for these concerns as quickly as possible. Liaise with all adults, family and services where needed.

- Well placed interventions such as Lego therapy, and emotional literacy where necessary.

- Know when a child's needs require outside support and a referral to CAMHS – not everything can be solved in-house or by hoping it will go away over time.

Bullying, grooming, radicalisation and abuse.

- Ensure that pupils build resilience in staying safe and making safe decisions online.

- Educate parents about the risks associated with social media. Educate adults in what to look for.

- Actively engage with families who allow young pupils to have phones.

Strive to create a secure utopia

- Calming music or art in the corridors.
- An expectation of tranquil transitions within the building.
- Use lockers for belongings – safe, tidy and secure.
- Adults modelling correct behaviour and communication between one another and to others.
- A sense of understanding and security to their needs – MDAs and LSAs trained to ensure smooth lunchtimes in which people 'listen'. One person not engaged within the school's approach can be significantly damaging.

Stability and clarity in behaviour

- Most importantly – have the children own the policy and know clear, consistent consequences for unwanted actions, but also routes for praise and reward – the clearer it is, the safer they feel.
- Proactively tackle bullying and issues around diversity, including guest speakers, lessons and assemblies.
- Ensure adults and pupils are aware of individuals' triggers and develop a respect and understanding that we are all different but all deserve the same e.g. respect, care, attention, understanding, emotional support.

The PROGRESS approach is the foundation for a wider, multi-tiered strategy. At Longwood Primary Academy, we work alongside Place2Be to provide a bespoke programme for our community.

Longwood's multi-tiered approach for mental health, wellbeing and the unknown

The PROGRESS approach is fundamental in developing an ethos to support those vulnerable. However, in order to effectively cater for the increasing numbers of children displaying, or at risk of, mental health issues, the school developed a multi-tiered approach to wellbeing. This encompassed the use of outside agencies, counselling, interventions, open door provision and whole school initiatives.

PLACE2 THINK	Outside agency input			Safe-guarding
open door sessions for teachers to discuss mental health and wellbeing for their class	EWHMS, SEND, Child Development Centre, family support services			including the close liaison with the safe guarding leader for a whole picture of the child
	1:1 Counselling with Place2Be		**Parent Support** 1:1 counselling with Place2Be	
	Group work (social and emotional skills) this includes the development of an individual's social circles	**High quality SEND interventions** increasing outcomes	**Family Support Officer** providing additional school-home relationship, links and training for parents	
	Wellness Centre A place for all pupils to come and talk to an adult or trained peer. Also a place to relax and to 'be'.	**Pupil Led Programmes** Programmes designed and run by pupils on feelings and solving problems, including playground buddies & programme leaders	**Place 2 Talk** Walk in sessions for pupils with concerns	
	INSIDE-OUTSIDE initiative* High quality diet and taking part in 'The Daily Mile'[8] to increase serotonin and awareness of mental health benefits		**Barrier Plans**** Knowing the children's barriers – creating a picture of the WHOLE person	
	High quality training and links for staff on Mental Health and Wellbeing School based and external specialists e.g. Place2Be, YoungMinds			
	High quality teaching Raising outcomes and opportunities			
	PROGRESS approach			

INSIDE-OUTSIDE Initiative* to ensure that we prepare our young for resilience we need to instill into them an understanding of the benefits in independently tackling depression. Two key areas that help in the increase of serotonin (the feel good hormone) are diet and exercise. A school that actively promotes the fact that exercise and a healthy life style will aid in feeling good can make a difference to individuals that may be susceptible to depression. An understanding of these benefits, coupled with the above provision, is essential in ensuring that children know where to go and what to do if they are feeling sad.

Barrier Plans** are used for all pupils with any disadvantage, from the label of 'Pupil Premium' and beyond. Instead of looking at what the school can currently offer, focus on the pupils first and then determine their needs and what the school *should* offer. These have been fundamental in knowing our children and combining all staff together to discuss individuals, giving a telling picture of individual needs.

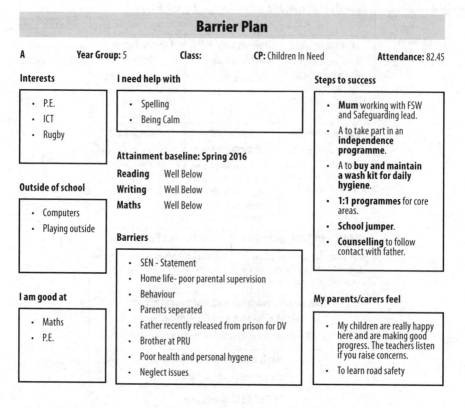

Barrier Plan

A   Year Group: 5   Class: CP: Children In Need   Attendance: 82.45

Interests
- P.E.
- ICT
- Rugby

Outside of school
- Computers
- Playing outside

I am good at
- Maths
- P.E.

I need help with
- Spelling
- Being Calm

Attainment baseline: Spring 2016

Reading   Well Below
Writing   Well Below
Maths   Well Below

Barriers
- SEN - Statement
- Home life- poor parental supervision
- Behaviour
- Parents seperated
- Father recently released from prison for DV
- Brother at PRU
- Poor health and personal hygene
- Neglect issues

Steps to success
- **Mum** working with FSW and Safeguarding lead.
- A to take part in an **independence programme**.
- A to **buy and maintain a wash kit for daily hygiene**.
- **1:1 programmes** for core areas.
- **School jumper**.
- **Counselling** to follow contact with father.

My parents/carers feel
- My children are really happy here and are making good progress. The teachers listen if you raise concerns.
- To learn road safety

Risk Factors… and the concealed

The Mental Health Foundation (2016) signposted certain risk factors that make some children and young people more likely to experience problems:

- having a long-term physical illness
- having a parent who has had mental health problems, problems with alcohol or has been in trouble with the law
- experiencing the death of someone close to them
- having parents who separate or divorce
- having been severely bullied or physically or sexually abused
- living in poverty or being homeless

- experiencing discrimination, perhaps because of their race, sexuality or religion
- acting as a carer for a relative, taking on adult responsibilities
- having long-standing educational difficulties.

However, there are those that are hidden, those that hide and internalise – not understanding their feelings or can comprehend that something is wrong until they do become one of the aforementioned statistics. Tackling Mental Health problems in school is one of the fundamental cornerstones to changing futures. It is our primary duty, to ensure academic achievement, and to actively create an ethos to support mental health and to clearly signpost one thing... help is here.

James Hollinsley, Head of School – Longwood Primary Academy

James Hollinsley is the Head of School at Longwood Primary Academy. James was previously the Lead Practitioner for SEND in a London borough and has extensive leadership experience in both secondary special and primary education. He is a practicing Ofsted Inspector and qualified SENCO.

@hollinsley

More effective use of Teaching Assistants

The role and impact of Teaching Assistants (TAs) has been under scrutiny for a while now. Research has shown that TAs can make little difference to the progress and attainment of pupils and in some instances that they can even have a detrimental effect. As is often the case with taking research headlines at face value however, this is not the whole story. When managed effectively, TAs who carry out specific interventions overseen by qualified staff can have a positive effect on the progress and attainment of pupils.

At Rosendale Primary School, we wanted to analyse the work of TAs in more detail in order to make some informed judgements about the work they do and the impact they have. We conducted a time and motion study of the class based activities of each of our 31 TAs. Every TA was observed for a whole day during their time in classrooms. Each 15-minute period throughout the day was assigned a score based on the following criteria:

Score 1 – TA being passive (watching the teacher teach) or carrying out activities such as tidying.

Score 2 – TA reacting to a teacher request during the lesson to help a pupil/group of pupils.

Score 3 – TA independently following a previously agreed plan/way of working to coach pupils, carry out intervention marking and/or play a role in behaviour management.

Score 4 – TA taking the initiative to make suggestions about children's learning to the teacher. For example explaining that a pupil required some re-teaching and then carrying this out when and where appropriate.

Given the investment made by schools in TAs (national spending circa £4.4 billion), schools must expect the majority of TA time to have a positive effect on children's learning. A predominance of scores 3 and 4 and a lack of scores 1 and 2 appearing in the results of the study would demonstrate this.

The results of the research we carried out were as follows:

Score 1 – 20% *

Score 2 – 3%

Score 3 – 63%

Score 4 – 14%

*The percentages are of the total amount of TA time in classrooms

According to these results 77% of TA time in our school is spent carrying out activities that have a positive impact on pupils' learning. The majority of this time is accounted for by activity planned for by the class teacher. The other 14% shows

TAs acting with autonomy in the best interests of the children. We were heartened by these results.

It was the 20% of time spent being passive and not contributing to positive outcomes for children that warranted action from the school's leadership team. We viewed this 20% as too much learning time not being used to its maximum potential.

At Rosendale we have now moved away from a model where TAs are passive participants in class, often sitting with lower attaining children, to one where they are more like co-teachers. This is evident in the following aspects of their role:

During independent learning

Our pupils spend up to 45 minutes each morning carrying out independent learning activities which have been planned by the class teacher. These are broadly activities involving pre teaching, over learning and responding to marking feedback. Instead of walking around the classroom providing help when it is asked for, TAs are now given specific (pupil premium) children to support. Each TA completes a weekly log reporting how they have made an impact on each of these children's learning. This is linked to their performance management targets.

When managing behaviour

Our time and motion study showed that most TAs would sit or stand at the back of the classroom when the teacher was delivering the learning. Sometimes they would sit next to a child who needed close supervision but this was not required in most classrooms. We have moved to a model where the TAs now sit or stand at the front of the classroom alongside the teacher. The school behaviour system (involving awarding red and green choices) is also located at the front of the classroom and TAs now manage this during whole class teaching.

Children can see the adults working in collaboration and that the TA is fundamental to behaviour management. The teacher can focus 100% of their effort on teaching and learning. Children with more significant behaviour issues are managed effectively with looks and annotations on the behaviour chart and are then spoken to by the teacher at a convenient time after the learning has been delivered.

When providing additional support

Where TAs deliver specific targeted interventions they can have a positive effect on children's learning. Most of our TAs continue to work in class under the direction of the teacher but some do take groups of children out of class for additional support. This support does not replace core lessons but is in addition to them. The programmes are well researched and ones which are well suited to our children's needs such as Units of Sound, Direct Phonics, Phonological Awareness

Training, Racing to English, Anger Management and Power of 2. TAs have time out of class to plan these sessions alongside the class teacher or SENDCo. The impact of these sessions is monitored by the SLT.

Ensuring that the TAs work closely with class teachers and are accountable for what they do has helped us to implement these new initiatives effectively.

The effective deployment of teaching assistants is a challenging one. This sector of staff is often proud and forthright, and initiatives to change or enhance the way they work need careful thought and precise implementation. A leadership team with good ideas and an expectation that they will be carried out is not enough. Changing the way large numbers of people work needs whole school co-operation and acceptance in order to achieve success and meaningful change.

Our profession is one that has always been besieged with the expectation to roll out initiative after initiative and so it is important to prevent the 'initiative fatigue' that can often occur when new governments take office, new headteachers arrive or when enthusiastic senior leaders try to make their mark! We need to work hard to combat the scepticism that often accompanies the next 'new idea'.

Getting it right at Rosendale was aided by acknowledging the 'diffusion of innovation theory'. The term originates from Everett M. Rogers' Diffusion of Innovations (1962). The term is often used to explain how new products are adopted by society but is also used to describe and explain organisational change.

When a new idea is mooted, there is a minority group (comprising about 14%) of the population who, after the innovators themselves, are the first to try out new ideas. This group tend to have an above-average level of education. For any new product to be successful, it must attract these early adopters, so that its acceptance or 'diffusion' moves quickly through the different groups; the early majority, late majority, and finally to the laggards.

It is important to acknowledge this theory because it is invariably applied to implementing new initiatives in school. Winning early adopters is often the easiest part. It is the continual and often long term drive that is needed to get the other 86% on board that is hard work. Without this 86%, any idea, however well it is backed up by research and is crucial to the core purpose and vision of the school, is doomed.

At Rosendale we worked very closely with the early adopter TAs who were able to influence the others effectively. They might not have been innovators themselves but by having their support and by affording them responsibility in delivering change, there came an accountability which helped us to make rapid improvements to learning. Teachers and leaders played a crucial role in this process by enabling training, by planning and monitoring interventions, and by assessing impact.

While TAs continue to account for large amounts of schools' budgets, this investment in teacher and leadership time is worthwhile. TAs delivering strategically targeted, well planned and monitored strategies and interventions can have a positive effect on children's learning. As leaders we need to enable this to happen.

Scott Palmer, Rosendale Primary School

Scott Palmer is a Deputy Headteacher at Rosendale Primary School. Scott worked in the restaurant, airline, health and psychiatric hospital industries before becoming a teacher in his late thirties. He has taught in every primary age range and was the SENDCo at Rosendale before becoming a member of the senior leadership team. He recently completed his NPQH.

Developing teachers to enable great learning for vulnerable pupils

The biggest driver of impact in any school system is what happens in the classrooms. The most important factor for any learner within a school is the quality of the teaching[27]. This is particularly true for disadvantaged and vulnerable learners who benefit most from high quality teaching.[28]

So what can we do as school leaders to enable great quality teaching?

Developing teachers to be great teachers is one of the most important things you can do as a school leader[29]. One teacher described how the process of collaborative enquiry, which encompassed the key aspects of effective professional development, transformed the way she worked with her class, her colleagues and one pupil in particular. "A girl who'd almost never existed for me in my PE lesson is now loving her lessons. She's even started coming to athletics club after school". At the same time, in the staffroom people were having "pedagogical conversations that simply wouldn't have happened before". Powerful professional learning helps teachers to reach and have an impact on their pupils, but also to empower them professionally.

Yet high quality teacher professional development is difficult to achieve and can easily slip down leaders' priority lists. We all have an untouched 'box of guilt' containing great ideas from different training sessions and courses we've been to that we will 'get around to one day'. We can probably also think of examples where great ideas have been diluted into quite token areas of practice. Similarly, it is not uncommon to have experienced a CPD session focused on generic needs, or generic pedagogy, that doesn't quite fit with our learners and our context and consequently its potential to impact on our learners remains untapped.

So what does professional learning look like when it is really supporting great teaching for vulnerable learners?[30]

---

27 Barber, M., Clark, M., and Whelan F. (2010) Capturing the leadership premium: how the world's top school systems are building leadership capacity for the future. London: McKinsey and Company.

28 www.suttontrust.com/wp-content/uploads/2011/09/2teachers-impact-report-final.pdf

29 Robinson, V.M.J., Lloyd, C., & Rowe, K.J. (2008). The Impact of Leadership on Student Outcomes: An analysis of the differential effects of leadership type. Educational Administration Quarterly, 44(5)635-674

30 Cordingley, P., Higgins, S., Greany, T., Buckler, N., Coles-Jordan, D., Crisp, B., Saunders, L., Coe, R. (2015) Developing Great Teaching: Lessons from the international reviews into effective professional development. Teacher Development Trust.

1. Powerful professional learning is driven by pupils' needs

This is something that is easy to assume is in place, but is actually often missing. A broad focus on a form of teaching practice or a general pupil need is not sufficient to really impact on pupil outcomes. Effective professional learning should include a real exploration of the learning needs of specific pupils and the contextualising, refining and adapting of practice that impacts on those pupils. There should be a clear understanding at the beginning of the process of what success would look like, specific to one's own pupils and their context.

A common picture for vulnerable learners is to focus on broad groups, such as those eligible for pupil premium, or those with different labels of learning needs, rather than to really diagnose the needs and experiences of specific pupils within your own class and context.

2. Participants evaluate the impact on pupils

To ensure that professional learning is impacting on pupils, the process needs to include regular opportunities to evaluate the impact on those particular pupils. There should be opportunities and tools built in to support formative assessment for continually evaluating the impact of practice on pupils. This includes assessing outcomes and work, but may also include more qualitative assessment from peer observations, for example.

3. It is collaborative, iterative and sustained

Professional learning should incorporate opportunities for colleagues to discuss and collaborate, and for peer support in general. Several heads are better than one, and allow for more challenge, dialogue and problem solving. Crucially though, this collaborative process needs to be sustained over time in order to see a real impact on practice and pupil learning. Teaching is a habit that we do day in and day out, and to change that habit we need a sustained focus, with multiple opportunities to discuss, review, evaluate and reflect.

4. Professional learning is underpinned by evidence and includes challenge and input from external expertise

It is surprisingly easy for professional learning opportunities to result in reinforcement of existing ideas and practice. To see a change in pupil outcomes and teacher practice, professional learning needs to include a challenge to existing understanding and practice. It is important to engage with external expertise to enable both challenge and support for teachers. Of course it is also crucial that teachers are engaging in evidence informed practice. This may be supported by external expertise, direct engagement and use of research, or in other ways. It is important to consider the evidence behind approaches when considering and deciding upon external expertise.

We know that vulnerable learners are too often disadvantaged in schools. Great teaching has a disproportionate benefit for them, and powerful professional learning helps not only these pupils succeed but helps teachers thrive too. We want all colleagues in schools to be supported and developed to reach those vulnerable and disadvantaged children, so that the ones "who never really exist" can begin to "love their lessons", thrive and achieve. With powerful professional learning for all colleagues, we can bring a real transformation to pupils' learning in school.

Bridget Clay, Network Programme Manager – Teacher Development Trust

Bridget Clay leads the TDT Network at the Teacher Development Trust, the national charity for CPD. Bridget is a former teacher who provides advice and consultancy for schools and organisations around effective professional learning and is a regular media contributor.

@bridget89ec

It takes a village ... to raise a child

Adoptive parents experience an exciting but rapid and demanding learning curve when their children are first placed. Like all new parents they may have some problems adjusting to parenthood no matter how much they welcome the child's arrival. Often this is the time when services and support may disappear. If the child/ren were of school age there may be 1 or 2 PEP meetings until the adoption order is granted, but these soon cease alongside home visits. The perception from society is typically that the term 'adopted from care' draws a line on the past and that the children's lives will be transformed with immediate effect.

So how can educational settings best advocate adopted children?

I have selected three themes which I believe from the perspective of both a professional in education and an adoptive parent highlight best practice for adopted children. These simple steps will most probably benefit all children.

1. Starting school or starting a new school

Demonstrate that you are a school which is high on nurture, tight on structure and flexible about individual needs.

- Invite the family to meet the teacher, pop in informally, for example, for story time, etc. Let the child explore their classroom and see that it is fun and safe. Be flexible with transition whatever their age.

- Create a personalised booklet for the child to view prior to their initial visit including photographs of key staff, areas like their classroom, cloakroom, toilets, school office and the dining hall.

- Teacher and therapist Louise Bomber recommends the appointment of a sensitive key adult as a substitute attachment figure for the child in school. The key adult is additional to the class teacher and while the teacher may change every year, the key adult should be available to the child for at least two to three years. The key adult is often a classroom assistant, who has time to work with the child, and the ability to stay regulated when the child is dysregulated. If the child is invited to rehearse and role play situations that are likely to crop up, play provides a safe way to practise new skills and situations.

- Encourage the child to bring in transitional objects and sensory reminders of home to help the child feel safe. They may need reassurance that their adoptive parent will return each day to collect them from school.

- Providing a sensory-comforting safe space in the classroom (and elsewhere in school) can allow children who become anxious or over stimulated to take a few minutes out to get regulated.

- Familiarise the child with what's coming next and when things start and finish. Produce a visual timetable of how each school day is broken up, include home time. Stick to the timetable or provide advance notice if a visitor, visit or other change will take place.

- Arrange an exit strategy before a crisis – Schools need to be aware that children with a trauma history are likely to struggle with separation and stress. Agree a pre-arranged exit strategy to prevent meltdowns, shamed-based behaviours or even school refusal. These can be simple breaks from school that allow attachments with family to grow –perhaps staggered attendance, a regular afternoon out with Dad mid-week, or some other arrangement that suits the child's attachment needs.

2. Building relationships and trust

Schools and adoptive parents should aim to develop strong, positive and direct links as effective exchange of information about matters relating to pupils' education and well-being is essential.

- Invite the adoptive parent/s to share a genogram of the birth family and the newly adopted family. Adopted children may have two sets of parents and may have brothers and sisters living elsewhere. There may be no or very little information.

- Be clear about contact arrangements. Their birth family and foster carers may still be a very real part of their lives through ongoing face to face contact and this can be unsettling at times. Letterbox contact can also unsettling. Dates will be useful for teachers and designated leads to be aware of. If birth family members do not adhere to contact arrangements this can lead to further feelings of rejection.

- If the child engages you in conversation about their birth family, listen and acknowledge that they are significant people in the child's life. Do not judge. Be open and honest.

- Establish an on-going dialogue with the adoptive parent/s. Demonstrate that you are an 'Adoption friendly school'. Find out what support they would like. Work together to support the child through times of changes at school. Typical flashpoints include: the start and end of term; if the teacher, teaching assistant, key adult or friend is absent; PPA; moving child or friend to a different seat; start and end of day; break and lunchtimes; school visits; residentials; any change to the timetable or routine; moving up to a new class or change of setting.

- Children with attachment difficulties are often branded 'attention seeking', because they can't bear to be left alone and need to know they are held in mind at all times. Best practice is to check in with the child at regular intervals. Teachers and TAs should use sensory reminders of their presence like wearing a jingly bracelet or a specific perfume/aftershave.

3. Curriculum Design

Is your curriculum adoption friendly? In the large majority of schools the curriculum is based on the premise that family life is good and so it is littered with topics about babyhood, family trees, personal timelines, local culture, and traditional family units. Schools/academies can minimise possible distress by publishing their curriculum overviews on their websites. This will enable adoptive parents to see which topics are coming up and when. This can be approached in two ways:

- Liaise with the parents about adapting topics to respect the experiences of every child in the class. Capture their views on aspects of your curriculum from an adoption perspective.

- Prepare the child in advance by providing strategies and cover stories. This is better than removing the child from class when topics arise, as this only encourages avoidance of painful subjects and can draw attention to the child.

Additional tips

- Watch your language! The use of language is so important, two examples, use the term 'birth parent' not 'real parent'. Use 'animal sponsorship' – The idea of 'adopting' abused or abandoned animals can give offensive and confusing messages to adopted children.

- Recognise that children who have been abused may be reluctant to remove their clothes in company. Provide a plan with adoptive parents.

- Demonstrate that your workforce have received 'Stonewall Training' to ensure that diversity is interwoven into the curriculum and features in Collective Worship. As a result, your whole school ethos is sensitive to difference in families, this includes: adoption, transgender, LBGT. Many adopted parents are in same sex relationships.

- Are pupil voice groups representative of your school community, are there opportunities for adopted children to lead? Are barriers removed to enable adopted children to participate in extra-curricular provision?

Liz Bramley, Headteacher – Oakdene Primary School

Liz Bramley is the Executive Head Teacher of Oakdene Primary School and a National Leader of Education.

Liz has a proven track record of leading a school to Outstanding, Oakdene has been a consistently high performing school for the last 10 years. She has considerable experience of working in schools serving disadvantaged communities placed in Ofsted categories to move to good or outstanding. Liz was a member of the 2015 TSC Fellowship Commission and is instrumental in driving forward the school led system through her work.

Liz's particular areas of expertise are in provision of high quality Early Years' experience, promotion of high achievement for all across the primary phase, and developing a rich, inspirational and memorable curriculum based on local community need.

Liz has recently collaborated with North East schools to produce a series of case studies 'What are little boys made of?' This work promotes strategies which are proving highly successful to ensure that boys can meet and exceed a Good level of development exiting Early Years.

Liz has a strong belief that through promoting high aspirations, giving support, challenge, care and respect and creating strong teamwork excellent teaching and learning will be achieved.

@Liz_Bramley

Waiting for the right time to speak; knowing you'll be heard

Whatever a child's background it should be clear to them that they have the power to influence learning in the classroom. At Woodrow we aim to build a school community of discussion.

Before I came to Woodrow this was the level of ignorance evident in my thinking; an ignorance borne out of lack of experience. I didn't realise the impact that high levels of vulnerable and /or disadvantaged children have on resources, services, time and energy. I knew of patches of poverty and rural deprivation – a lack of access to services. But I didn't know enough about schools centred in communities where there are the vulnerable[31] and the disadvantaged on a large scale.

Disadvantage does not always follow vulnerable and vice versa but one can often be found with the other. Disadvantage also means children are more likely to start school with a language delay[32]. A key part of the challenge we face is to address this. We have an ethos of nurture and great relationships are vital: there are lots of smiles and wide ranging opportunities (bringing the seaside to land locked Redditch) and off-site visits (Universities, theatres, museums, cities, hills). We also give them opportunity through having a voice.

At Woodrow, talk is central to sophisticated sequences of lessons. Lots of talk. Purposeful talk. Talking for meaning and explanation, talking to predict, suppose, ponder and wonder. This is where using the Mantle of the Expert[33] approach is key to developing talk. It is not an opportunity for frivolous loose talk. As Dorothy Heathcote, the first lady of classroom drama, memorably said to a group of startled teachers and researchers: "Do not natter; in Mantle we do not natter."

In school, children wait for the right time to speak. Children and adults are given time and space to think and respond. We may probe and challenge further. We learn how to ask questions, as do the children. A simple smile and a nod might elicit a nugget of gold.

Part of our planning is to create opportunities where speaking, talking, discussing, debating, pondering all play a pivotal role in a narrative constructed together. As teachers, we have all been on courses, in staff rooms, at lectures when questions

---

31 Deep End Report 12. (2010). Working together for vulnerable children and families. General Practitioners at the Deep End, available at; www.gla.ac.uk/medi/media_183114_en.pdf

32 Law et al 2013 Early Language Delays in the UK available at www.ncl.ac.uk/cflat/news/documents/Lawetal2013EarlyLanguageDelaysintheUK.pdf

33 The Mantle of the Expert is a dramatic-inquiry based approach to teaching and learning invented and developed by Professor Dorothy Heathcote at the University of Newcastle upon Tyne in the 1980s. The big idea is that the class do all their curriculum work as if they are an imagined group of experts. See www.mantleoftheexpert.com

are asked and there is a deathly tornado of silence swirling through the room feeding our discomfort. At Woodrow we work hard to ensure silence is not be feared. At our school we want the children to welcome silence and a moment to think. We have created a culture where everyone in school can speak or be silent in safety. They will not be laughed at and what they say will be respected.

Some children talk more than others; this doesn't mean the quieter ones shouldn't be heard or acknowledged. Their many ways of communicating are always recognised and nurtured. When children use drama they do so with confidence. From the start of nursery children are encouraged to have and share a point of view. They prepare arguments, make phone calls, speak with a client, report on their work constantly deepening understanding.

This approach has to start from the beginning in Nursery and Reception where children suffer with poor receptive language. A language rich environment is critical. Language needs to be bursting from the ceilings and the walls. Stories, imagination, drama and invention are some ways to achieve this.

We invest in speech and language. We screen for Receptive Language. We have a speech therapist in school for two days a week who works with pupils and trains staff. We teach children to talk and we continually practice.

With our families, every conversation on the playground is an investment. We need to work with parents too. We run workshops where communication is central and visitors know they will not be talked at or patronised. We want an environment where parents will feel they want to return, knowing their voices will be heard.

Richard Kieran, Woodrow First School

Richard is Headteacher of Woodrow First School in Redditch. He has been teaching children and adults in the UK and abroad for 25 years and is happier in a classroom than on his backside in the chair in his office.

@RKieran

Cracks in the Pavement –
The Disadvantaged and University

The girl walking home from school was avoiding the cracks in the pavement.

It was her way of avoiding looking in the windows of the houses she passed and shutting out the envy she felt towards the people who lived there. Sometimes she imagined stepping on a crack and falling into it, into a different life altogether. A life where she was collected from school by a parent. A life where she could catch a school bus with a group of friends. A life where she did not have to sit in lessons with pupils who did not want to work, or where others were allowed to steal your belongings and spit in your hair.

She walked alone as her parents could not meet her from school. Her mother did not have time; she was at home looking after her younger siblings. Her dad did not have time; he worked shifts and would not be home from work until late in the evening.

At home she had nowhere to complete her homework. She would be kept awake until late by her younger brother and if she wanted to change her library book she would have to go to the library alone.

When she reached eighteen, the girl had aspirations, she had good A level results. She chose a university from a long list of places she had never visited; Leeds, Hull, Manchester, Bristol and Brighton. If she wanted a university education, she would have to learn how to overcome the obstacles along the way.

It did not matter that she was self-motivated, had good time management skills, had obtained good results without the aid of a personal tutor. It did not matter that she had managed to navigate the UCAS process alone. She was still perilously close to falling down one of the cracks she had been so careful to avoid. She would have to learn rules which required her to leave her home and its values. She would have to learn to talk about ski trips, play hockey and eat meals in restaurants. There is a chance that she would decide not to go at all.

How can schools make sure that 'white working class' students make it to University?

1. Take the time to understand the barriers, as these may not always be obvious. For many there is simply a lack of guidance about higher education. Even more so if no one in the immediate family has experience of going to University.

2. Provide 'widening participation' programmes where students are supported with the logistics of travelling to University amongst other things.

3. Ensure programmes focus on a wide range of University experiences. They should not just include Oxbridge and Russell group Universities. Programmes should expose students to a choice of University options. Links can be established early in Primary Schools with outreach and in reach programmes.

4. Put in place mentoring programmes which can be offered by different professionals with different types of experience. They can talk about what University life was like for them.

5. Encourage membership of sports teams or music groups which can help students build relationships with adults who are not teachers and support them in developing the skills needed to work as part of a team. Often the opportunities that come along with joining these types of groups will help students link with people outside of their usual community and provide a safe forum for discussion.

6. Provide opportunities to discuss the types of career an undergraduate degree will lead to. Consider that some courses may offer more scope and provide a clearer career direction, and that some sandwich courses may be able to provide additional financial support through a work placement.

7. Build cultural capital through all aspects of school life.

8. Make it clear that not all universities require or need students to live away from home.

9. Support students with their transition from sixth form to university, in the same way that transition programmes are built for students moving from primary to secondary school. Include support around life skills, managing money and planning meals, as well as working within groups and getting along with others.

10. Teach that a university education is much more than just about getting a job. A great education enriches lives in ways more than just the financial.

Michelle Haywood, Entrust Education Service

Michelle is a SEN & Inclusion Service Manager & SEND Consultant at Entrust Education Service. She is an associate of the University of Wolverhampton.

@michhayw

How support staff can improve outcomes for vulnerable learners

Good teaching is fundamental to improving learner outcomes. But if school leaders focus on teachers alone, schools can miss opportunities to improve outcomes for pupils, particularly those that are vulnerable learners. Proper deployment and fully utilising the knowledge and skills of support staff (who make up 50% of the workforce) would create huge opportunities.

The evidence for the effective use of Teaching Assistants (TAs) is increasingly positive. The Education Endowment Foundation (EEF) has published the results of seven randomised control trials (RCTs) of TA led projects.

The results of the first six led Jonathan Sharples, the EEFs Senior Researcher to say:

"... *all six* projects involving Teaching Assistant led literacy/numeracy interventions have shown positive impacts on pupil learning, typically adding around three to four additional months' progress. Encouragingly, there are signs that these interventions disproportionately benefit low attaining and pupils eligible for Free School Meals, and so could be effective approaches to 'narrow the gap'. Having worked in communicating the findings from research for over ten years, this is by far the most consistent, positive set of results I have seen for real-world RCTs."[34]

These projects and other research show that joint planning, high quality training and support from teachers and senior leaders is crucial to making TA interventions work. Also, whilst TAs have a positive effect on teachers' workload, pupil attention and class disruption, those that are poorly trained, unsupported and are asked to do general or undirected one to one work may well not benefit learning outcomes at all.[35] This is a leadership issue.

Support staff provide invaluable pastoral support. Learning Mentors are crucial in helping pupils develop coping strategies, enhance their motivation, raise their aspirations and re-engage them in learning. They can be skilled in assessing the complex issues that lie behind problems with learning and achievement. These could include things such as bereavement, lack of confidence/low self-esteem, low expectations, mental health issues, relationship difficulties, bullying, peer pressure and family issues; some students face **all** these barriers.

Parent Support Advisers/Education Welfare Officers can work with pupils and families to resolve poor attendance, overcome barriers to learning, help parents support their children's learning and assist families to access funding. And

34 Sharples J: Education Endowment Foundation: Six of the best: how our latest reports can help you support teaching assistants to get results educationendowmentfoundation.org.uk/news/six-of-the-best-how-our-latest-reports-can-help-you-support-teaching-assist/

35 Blatchford P. et al: Deployment and impact of support staff project. Department for Children, Schools and Families August 2009. Research Brief DCSF- RB148

Family Support Workers are increasingly being employed by schools to assist families with particular needs and help them develop parenting skills; working closely with social workers, educational psychologists and others.

But it isn't just classroom and direct support workers who help vulnerable learners. In the most effective schools, the whole school workforce is a team. Lunchtime staff should regularly engage with vulnerable children, ensure they aren't missing meals and know to eat regularly and healthily. Midday supervisors can look after nervous and shy pupils in the playground, helping them to integrate and play. There are always opportunities to develop children's language. Reports to pastoral leaders on diet or isolation are hugely important in overall care.

Administrative staff can assist parents in completing forms that give families access to funds and support. But these colleagues must be valued. The pejorative term 'back office staff' ignores the invaluable cross cutting work that administrative staff do.

One of the most vulnerable groups of children are refugees. Across the country support staff are leading the way in acting as coordinators of support packages to help integrate pupils who may have no English. They may have no friends and sometimes no family. One school[36] highly regarded by the Home Office for their work with Syrian children and their families, has a teaching assistant led integration project. From day one they create a relaxed atmosphere, offering flowers and welcome cards, simple but effective in making the families feel wanted by their new school community.

As the lead TA says: 'I remember the first day the children started school. They arrived with a local authority education officer. They smiled and looked nervous but the fact the children had no English was not a barrier. We used gestures, pictures and even Google Translate helped a little. However we avoided using PAD as we wanted to communicate with them directly. The children's determination and resilience to succeed was amazing. As the weeks went by their English developed through small group work and integration with other children in lessons. Soon they were teaching me their language and culture. I regularly met with parents and support workers to update them about their children's progress and wellbeing they are settling into the community."

TAs work closely with teachers, other support staff and LA colleagues in building a local support network. The school hosts ESOL classes for their parents and those from partner primary schools to create a wider learning community, building trust and confidence.

When a new group of refugee families arrived, the school involved the Syrian children who were already settled. This meant the children learned even quicker. The lead TA also used the children to help deliver CPD for teachers on effective teaching and learning strategies.

---

36 Due to the sensitivity of this work the school and staff are not named

They said, "Pupils give back to us by teaching us about resilience, respect, kindness and especially hope. Their hope for a better future has not been destroyed, even if their country has been ravaged by war."

Innovative and flexible approaches like this highlight the immense value of support staff. A pool of untapped talent skills that could unlock the potential of some of the most valuable vulnerable learners. Schools should unleash their 50 percent.

Jon Richards

Jon Richards, is Head of Education for UNISON, covering a quarter of a million support staff working in schools. Jon sits on the DfE's Education Forum, represents the European Public Services Union (EPSU) at the EU Social Dialogue for Education and EPSU on Public Service International's Education and Cultural Support Workers Network.

@tiddymoke

Supporting struggling readers at Key Stage 3

With the introduction of a new primary curriculum and statutory assessments, secondary schools are now finding themselves with an increasing number of children arriving who are 'working below' the national expected standard for reading at the end of Key Stage 2. All too often, an intervention is deployed as the first defence to enable pupils to catch up. However, there is risk that the intervention will have little impact if it has not been carefully chosen and tailored to meet the needs of the learners. Too often it is a case of what is available in school, rather than what the pupil needs.

There are several reasons why a young person may still be struggling with reading upon entry to Key Stage 3:

- Difficulty decoding means poor word recognition skills. Whilst this could be the result of a learning difficulty, there can be other reasons such as an intermittent hearing impairment (which maybe undiagnosed). It could be periods of absence or repeatedly relocating and moving schools. This learner will need a structured, phonics-based intervention which teaches the skills of decoding.

- Difficulty with inference, deduction and authorial intent. Difficulties of this nature are sometimes found amongst pupils with a communication and interaction disorder, such as ASD. In such cases, learners with these needs require a different type of reading intervention. It may be overseen by a Speech and Language Therapist.

- Difficulties with language acquisition. A report carried out in 2013 by Newcastle University on behalf of Save the Children concluded that children from the most disadvantaged groups have lower language skills than their more advantaged peers.[37] A learner with a limited vocabulary will need an intervention designed to increase word knowledge in addition to the explicit teaching of topic related vocabulary and exposure to language rich environments.

The SEN Code of Practice 2014 (Clause 6:13) makes it clear that slow progress and low attainment do not necessarily mean that a child can be labelled 'SEN'. Therefore, it is important that the first response to any area of weakness is high quality teaching with classroom teachers carrying out regular assessments to ensure lessons are adapted to meet the needs of all learners. Additional interventions, judiciously used, must supplement and not replace quality, teacher led instruction in the classroom.

If it is decided that a pupil does require an additional intervention, this must be carefully matched to the young person's needs. It should be delivered by

---

37 www.ncl.ac.uk/cflat/news/documents/Lawetal2013EarlyLanguageDelaysintheUK.pdf

a practitioner who is trained in programmes that have been independently evaluated for effectiveness. The Dyslexia-SpLD Trust provide useful links to the research at www.interventionsforliteracy.org.uk

The selection of any intervention must be driven by the following questions:

- What difficulties are we aiming to address?
- What outcomes do we want to see at the end of the intervention?
- How will we know if these have been achieved?

To avoid a reading intervention becoming a "bolt-on", teachers must be aware of the content and outcomes of each session so that learning can be integrated into whole class teaching, thus providing a cohesive experience for the learner.

There are several practical steps that the classroom teacher and the wider school can take to enhance language and reading development:

- Ensure that the young person has had a recent eye test and hearing check.
- Facilitate access to suitable reading materials and ensure that regular reading takes place at home and at school.
- Make sure pupils know how to use the school library. Have books in the classroom which pupils can borrow.
- Encourage pupils and their families to visit book sales and introduce a voucher scheme using Pupil Premium funding for the purchase of books.
- When reading and studying texts, always check for understanding; give pupils post-it notes so that they can jot down words they don't understand. Never assume a word is understood, particularly if it may be little used in present day contexts. A recent group reading session of a short biographical introduction to the poet Ted Hughes revealed that many Year 6 pupils did not know the meaning of the words "newsagent", "gamekeeper" and "gooseberry".
- Use a search engine during reading sessions to show images of unfamiliar words. This will help embed the learning.
- Provide as many opportunities as possible for talk in 'out of class' contexts. Some schools now have systems in place for lunch where staff and pupils sit together and talk. Encourage participation in extra-curricular clubs which will further provide language rich environments.
- Ensure that transition work between primary and secondary school (and at subsequent stages), does not just consist of activities to ensure pupils are socially and emotionally prepared for the move. It should also include opportunities for clear professional dialogue to take place between all those who know the young person best. This ensures that strengths, difficulties and barriers to learning can be addressed and careful planning for the next stage can take place.

Transition is a challenge for all pupils, but even more so for the young person arriving at secondary school as a struggling reader. Interventions can play an important part in helping pupils to catch-up. But the essential task is gaining knowledge of each learner's difficulties and gaps in learning. This must be the first course of action when tailoring appropriate provision to meet individual needs.

Rachel Rossiter, SENCO – Horringer Court, The Bury Trust

Rachel is a teacher and SENCo in a 9-13 school which is part of an All-Through Trust in Suffolk. Before qualifying, Rachel was a Teaching Assistant and she frequently reflects upon her experiences in a support role to inform her practice and plan provision for the young people in her setting.

@rachelrossiter

Improving educational outcomes for Black, Asian and Minority Ethnic (BAME) pupils

'No child should be expected to cast off the language and culture of the home as he crosses the school threshold, nor to live and act as though school and home represent two totally separate and different cultures which have to be kept firmly apart...'

The Bullock Report 1975

Our schools are becoming increasingly diverse. This is not only in terms of ethnicity but also linguistically, culturally and religiously. The latest census figures show that approximately 30% of the pupil population is from BAME backgrounds. In some cities such as London and Birmingham BAME pupils are now in the majority, with the pupil population being much younger than that of society at large.

Improvements in the attainment of BAME pupils have been much lauded by policy makers and commentators. The definitive reasons for this are still largely unexplored. The academic Simon Burges[38] cites the higher ethnic composition of London's schools being a major factor in contributing to the higher attainment seen in London's education system. He attributes this to the fact that *'...the children of immigrants typically have high aspirations and ambitions, and place greater hopes in the education system than the locals do'*. It is indeed the case that many BAME pupils perform much better in London compared to other areas in England. In fact, the higher concentration of BAME pupils in London means that many BAME groups nationally now perform better than average. One of the major success stories in recent years is that of Bangladeshi heritage pupils. This is largely due to the impressive attainment seen in places such as Tower Hamlets and other London local authorities, where there is a high concentration of Bangladeshi community members. This has led to national attainment for this group increasing too. However, my own analysis has shown that although there is a positive picture emerging of improved standards generally and specifically in London this is not the case for all BAME groups. Six BAME groups are still underperforming (Gypsy, Roma & Travellers, any other white background, Pakistani, white and black Caribbean, black Caribbean and any other black background) and even though there have been some improvements for these groups the gaps in attainment over time have remained the same.

Indeed the attainment of these groups varies considerably across regions and LAs and in-group variation is also a feature dependent on the different languages spoken by pupils within specific ethnic groups.[39]

---

38 'Understanding the success of London's schools' by Simon Burgess. October 2014 Working Paper No. 14/333.

39 'Language Diversity and Attainment in Secondary Schools', Demie et al, Lambeth Education Research and Statistics, May 2016

Looking at the disaggregated data we also know that social class has an impact across all ethnic groups, as does gender, but class itself has a more of an impact on White British pupils than other ethnic groups, despite many BAME groups having higher levels of deprivation as measured by eligibility for FSM. Interestingly very little research has been undertaken to consider the reasons for this considerable in-group variation within the White British group. One of the reasons posited for the socio-economic gaps being much narrower in BAME groups is because of the fact that non-FSM BAME groups tend to be much less prosperous than the White non-FSM group.

So in order to improve outcomes for BAME groups not currently performing well, and to address the high variations in attainment across the country for different BAME groups what can schools do?

• **Focus on 'intersectionality' when monitoring tracking and attainment data**

Instead of just looking at binary indicators such as FSM, gender, ethnic or EAL gaps look at how these can come together to impact on certain groups of pupils to disadvantage them further and consider how their needs can met in a holistic manner.

• **Be aware of unconscious teacher bias**

It is easy for all of us to form certain unconscious stereotypes of certain groups of pupils and thereby overlook the needs of pupils within that group or confirm our expectations of them. Research by Gillborn *et al*[40] showed that black Caribbean pupils were less likely to be entered for the higher tiers of GCSE examination peers by their teachers, meaning that there was cap placed on their attainment before they had even taken the examination. Strand's analysis[41] of the Longitudinal Study of Young People in England (LSYPE) indicates a White British–Black Caribbean achievement gap at age 14 which cannot be accounted for by socio-economic variables or a wide range of contextual factors. He concludes that *'the results indicate that Black Caribbean students are systematically under represented in entry to the higher tiers relative to their White British peers...'* and that *'differential entry to test tiers provides a window on teacher expectation effects which may contribute to the achievement gap'.* Dr Tammy Campbell's analysis[42] showed that on average, children placed in higher streams are judged and assessed disproportionately favourably, and children in lower streams at a disproportionately lower level. Moreover, her analyses show that certain groups are over-represented in lower streams, and under-represented in the highest groupings. Campbell

40 'Rationing Education: Policy, Practice, Reform and Equity' by Gillborn, D. & Youdell, D. (2000) Buckingham: Open University Press
41 'The white British-black Caribbean achievement gap: tests, tiers and teacher expectations'. By Strand, Steve. (2012) British Educational Research Journal, Vol.38 (No.1).
42 'Selected at seven: The relationship between teachers' judgments and assessments of pupils, and pupils' stream placements' by Tammy Campbell June 2014, Institute of Education.

states *'I want to stress that this isn't something unique to teachers. It's human nature. Humans use stereotypes as a cognitive shortcut and we're all prone to it.'*

- **Ensure that the school reflects the diversity of its pupil population**

As early as 1975 the Bullock Report[43] recognised the importance of incorporating the lived experiences and backgrounds of all children when it recommended that *'No child should be expected to cast off the language and culture of the home as he crosses the school threshold, nor to live and act as though school and home represent two totally separate and different cultures which have to be kept firmly apart. The curriculum should reflect many elements of that part of his life which a child lives outside school...'* Bearing in mind that pupils only spend approximately 15% of their time in school and the remaining 85% with family and friends, it is imperative that schools consider how they can build on the learning in the home environment.

- **Ensure all pupils feel safe, settled and secure**

All schools are judged on how well they safeguard pupils. There are, however, some negative experiences that BAME pupils can suffer without schools or their teachers even knowing, particularly when pupils are in the minority. Cline *et al*'s research[44] showed that a significant proportion of BAME pupils reported race-related name calling or verbal abuse at school or while travelling to and from school. Furthermore, no school in his sample had a fully developed strategy for preparing pupils through the curriculum for life in a diverse society. Bearing in mind the current political climate which is quite hostile to immigrants and by default BAME and Muslim communities this has resulted in an increase in requests for counselling from children and young people experiencing racist and religiously motivated bullying in schools.[45]

Sameena Choudry, Equitable Education

Sameena is the founder of Equitable Education www.equitableeducation.co.uk which focuses on closing the attainment gaps for different groups of vulnerable children who are at 'risk of underachieving'. Sameena started her career as a teacher and has worked as a lecturer, ITE tutor, senior leader, examiner and more recently in senior officer roles in three LAs. She is also a trained Ofsted Inspector.

@equitableEd

---

43 'A language for life' – The Bullock Report 1975
44 'Minority Ethnic Pupils in Mainly White Schools' by Cline et al 2002, DfES Research Report RR365
45 'Healing a divided Britain: The need for a comprehensive race equality strategy'. Equality and Human Right's Commission 2016 www.equalityhumanrights.com/sites/default/files/healing_a_divided_britain_-_the_need_for_a_comprehensive_race_equality_strategy_final.pdf

Access to the community of educated citizens: The importance of what we learn

Michael Oakeshott wrote that *"as civilized human beings, we are the inheritors neither of an inquiry about ourselves and the world, nor of an accumulating body of information, but of a conversation, begun in the primeval forests and extended and made more articulate in the course of centuries. It is a conversation which goes on both in public and within each of ourselves."*[46]

One may put a pupil in a chemistry laboratory, or give them the richest works of 19th century literature, and tell them they are free. However they cannot use that freedom. But if the pupil is inducted into the subject-specific conversation, handed down through the ages of human progress, they can participate in, challenge, and even undermine that conversation.

This applies to chemistry, to literature, to history, and even to democracy itself. For if one is unable to understand the assumed knowledge that educated people take for granted, one is unable to understand newspaper headlines or political broadcasts. One cannot participate as a member of the community of educated citizens. And hence one's life is absent of much that gives joy, beauty and humanity.

It is an entitlement for **all** people to enter the community of educated citizens. It is our job to provide a curriculum that allows access to the knowledge that enables one to join this community.

Subjects are not a random way of dividing up the curriculum. They have emerged as a way of organising the curriculum from our expanding knowledge of the world. The important differences between more hierarchical subjects such as mathematics and physics and more cumulative subjects, arguably such as history and literature demand that we consider the structure and sequence of knowledge in each subject carefully. It further demands that we respect the boundaries of subjects and their traditions.

When referencing vulnerability, school leaders too often start at a pupil's existing experience, perhaps citing 'relevance' to 'engage' the pupil in school, or because of a lack of belief driven by natural cognitive biases – humans routinely look for shortcuts to make assessments and being from the wrong family is one such shortcut. The effect is a tremendous 'dumbing down' of the education that child receives, dictated by circumstance or demographic. **All** pupils are entitled to have their knowledge broadened by school – for schooling to go beyond the experiences that they would otherwise have received. This argument is not won for most pupils, but it is all the more in its infancy when

---

46 Michael Oakeshott, Rationalism in Politics and Other Essays

referencing 'disadvantaged', 'SEN' or 'EAL' pupils. Too often, phrases like 'high expectations for all' in actuality exclude those with these labels, either implicitly or explicitly. More explicitly, too many appear to regularly lack the entitlement to study subjects allowing them access to the knowledge educated people take for granted. Vocational or technical qualifications are taken by a disproportionate number of these pupils prior to 16, and in some cases are introduced explicitly for pupils with *multiple labels of vulnerability*.

I am persuaded by Amanda Ripley's book *The Smartest Kids in the World*[47] that when we account for a child's background this can be counter-productive and lower expectations, so we should be aware of this. I follow Cristina Iannelli's exposition in *The Role of School Curriculum in Social Mobility*[48] that the biggest factor that separated the performance of similar pupils at grammar schools in comparison with other schools was the content of the curriculum, and further this longitudinal study illustrates that this difference becomes more pronounced as former pupils get older. We are hence not dealing with examination results, or immediate job prospects, but life chances alongside access to that that is of beauty. By denying access to academic subjects and an academic curriculum, we are denying access to what has been passed on by humans and what makes us human. We are unintentionally *dehumanising*.

If we say **all** pupils we must mean all pupils. We must recognise the perils of training pupils for jobs before 16, and of a technocratic education that denies them beauty, awe and wonder. Identifying 'underachievement' at an early age. Studies show that teachers tended to perceive low-income children as less able than their higher income peers with equivalent scores on cognitive assessments[49], so this assessment shaping the curriculum is all the more criminal.

"Red" Ellen Wilkinson, whilst assuring the Labour conference of 1946 that secondary moderns would not be dumping grounds, privately despaired that the "real stuff" was going to just the 25% whilst the 75% were dumped in secondary modern schools[50]. We may have come some way since then, but the "real stuff" is definitively not going to at least the 25% labelled different versions of 'vulnerable'. A broad academic curriculum is an entitlement for everyone.

Via 'differentiation' of the curriculum, we risk denying access to an induction into subjects on the basis of the label of vulnerability. We hence determine that this label, often demographically obtained, destines the pupil to be excluded from this community. Excluded from the conversation handed down through the ages and manifested in the twenty-first century.

47   Ripley, Amanda, 'The Smartest Kids in the World', Simon and Schuster, 2013
48   Ianelli, Cristina (2013) 'The Role of School Curriculum in Social Mobility', British Journal of Sociology of Education, Volume 34
49   Campbell, Tammy (2013), 'Stereotyped at Seven? Biases in Teacher Judgement of Pupils' Ability and Attainment'
50   Beckett, Francis, 'Clem Atlee', Politico Publishing, 2007

This question about curriculum is a question of inclusion. For if one is excluded from the community of educated citizens, one is excluded for life.

Stuart Lock, Cottenham Village College

Stuart Lock is Headteacher of Cottenham Village College, a comprehensive school a few miles north of Cambridge.

@StuartLock

Relocation, relocation, relocation: Managing school transfer for high mobility families

Moving house, it is said, is one of life's more stressful experiences. For adults, the practical worries are short-lived, but the effects on children can be more profound, longer-lasting, and sometimes hidden. It takes time to accept a decision you have had no say in, which leads to the loss of friends and a familiar environment. Alongside the emotionally taxing process of adjustment, there is the apprehension of starting a new school.

While moving is not an entirely negative experience for most children[51], research suggest the impact of repeatedly relocating and moving schools at non-standard times is acute. Children who move home frequently are less likely to achieve in their formal Key Stage One assessments, compared with children who stay put[52]. And only 27% of pupils who move schools three times or more during their secondary school career achieve five A* – C GCSEs, compared to the national average of 60%[53].

Disadvantaged children are disproportionately represented in the statistics for in-year admissions. 61% of in-year movers are either eligible for the pupil premium, are identified as having special educational needs, or both[54]. Other groups exposed to the turbulence of regular relocation are those whose education, compared to others, is more likely to be disrupted by persistent absence and exclusion unrelated to moving house or school: those from Gypsy, Roma and Traveller communities; refugees; those in public care; or those whose parents/carers serve in the armed forces.

Given the impact of this confluence of factors, what can schools do to ease the difficulties caused by the transfer between schools and to ensure children from high mobility families make progress?

1. Guard against complacency Transient pupils are not guests to be 'hosted' before moving on again. At worst, indeterminate length of stay means schools contribute to the sense and effects of impermanence by withholding efforts and resources to address the educational, emotional and social effects of constant uprooting and resettlement. Every day these pupils are in your school matters; make them count.

2. Be proactive Make contact with families early. This will ease anxieties and demonstrate that your school is a welcoming and supportive environment. Specify what will happen and when. Relocation means families can go temporarily 'off

51 www.cls.ioe.ac.uk/shared/get-file.ashx?itemtype=document&id=3068
52 theconversation.com/moving-home-can-affect-your-childrens-health-and-education-62738
53 www.thersa.org/discover/publications-and-articles/reports/between-the-cracks/Download
54 www.thersa.org/discover/publications-and-articles/reports/between-the-cracks/Download

grid', so get as many means of contact as possible. Provide weekly updates and offer help. Some parents/carers also need support, so mediate with agencies (e.g. local authority) that can help.

3. Own the transfer process Take responsibility for overseeing transfers. Create a checklist of the essential documentation you require from the child's current school and a timeline against which key actions must be completed. Obtain a full chronology from all agencies involved, past and present. Be meticulous and chase relentlessly. Simplify the process for receiving important and sensitive information. Take the shortest possible path and avoid using families as conduits; absorb the anxiety and workload where possible. Develop a similar handover process to assist the transfer of children from your school to another setting.

4. Create a transfer team Have a small team to handle transfers to and from your school. Appoint a member of your office staff to collect data and act as the principle point of contact for everyone involved in the transfer. Create a link worker role to liaise with families, schools and agencies. Schools in local clusters or partnerships could share personnel, co-funded using pupil premium money. Appoint a transfer lead to be responsible for developing a learning package. This should be an experienced teacher who reports directly to the SLT.

5. Acclimatisation Organise frequent transfer visits. Begin by meeting the child in their current setting. This is important for those who experience anxiety, have an autism spectrum condition, or who may have difficulty trusting new adults. Consider making a short video introducing your school to share online[55]. If your school has a frequent intake of pupils from highly mobile families, consider an induction programme delivered by your transfer lead on a weekly or fortnightly basis. Having a regular, planned programme means you're not reactive when new pupils arrive.

6. Build the learning and support package Ask the child's current school for workbooks and assessments so you can construct a learning package to meet their attainment profile. 'Move anxiety' can affect outcomes, so if you need to carry out any formal assessments, allow time for settling-in first. Take advice from your staff about how they're coping and plan accordingly. Make provisions for secondary-aged learners to continue studying qualifications they have already started. New arrivals can be emotionally vulnerable, so ensure they can access well-being support from the link worker whenever necessary. Match a new pupil with a 'buddy' with a similar profile who can show them the ropes.

School is an essential constant in the lives of disadvantaged learners. It is important to recognise that high mobility means even these environments can become unstable. Every day these pupils do not attend school is as critical to their

---

55 Brampton Village Primary School's website has good examples of resources to help with transfer for children of service families brampton.cambs.sch.uk/our-school/new-children-welcome

life chances as the days that they do. Having robust routines to facilitate transfer can limit the worst effects of relocation and ensure these learners thrive and achieve.

Rob Webster, Researcher – Centre for Inclusive Education, UCL Institute of Education

> Rob Webster is a researcher at the UCL Institute of Education, where he also leads the Maximising the Impact of Teaching Assistants initiative. His work centres on using research to help schools improve how they meet the needs of disadvantaged learners.
>
> **www.maximisingtas.co.uk**
> **@maximisingTAs**

Young Carers

All too often, when asking a school how they support young carers, the response is, "we don't have any young carers in our school". In reality, this may actually mean 'we don't know if we have young carers in our school. This is unlikely to be the case and the result is that our education system too often misses the opportunity to support one of our most vulnerable groups of learners.

What is a young carer?

Being a young carer means you will be providing the practical and/or emotional care that an adult would normally provide. This may include doing jobs around the house, shopping, helping with personal care (bathing, getting dressed), giving medication, providing emotional support and looking after themselves or their siblings.

The impact of being a young carer can be profound. Any adult with experience of taking on a substantial caring role will, however they view the experience overall, often talk about how tiring, worrying or lonely it can be. Being a young carer can affect a young person in many ways – including social isolation, bullying, difficulties with school attendance and achievement, and physical and mental ill health themselves.

What can a school do?

The principles that underpin supporting young carers well are the same as they are for supporting all vulnerable groups. This is not surprising when they essentially relate to the culture of a great school. Schools that do well by young carers need:

- Fantastic teaching
- Relentless and shared ambition for every pupil
- High expectations for both attainment and readiness
- Systems that identify barriers (and aggregated barriers) and are solution focused
- To develop provision that meets needs (not the other way around)
- Reflective and evidence-based decision making
- To be a school which is characterised by positive relationships
- More fantastic teaching

As a system leader, I recognise that our support for young carers is not as well developed as it is for many other vulnerable groups. We need to be talking about the quality of support for young carers, sharing the approaches and practice that are having the greatest impact. But we also need to focus on overcoming the lack of understanding. We need to improve the identification of young carers. The current situation often reminds me of the stage that we had reached as a profession in relation to pupils with Special Educational Needs when I was a new teacher twenty years ago.

'We don't have any young carers'

It is always hard to accurately quantify the size of a group that is often hidden, but research conducted by the BBC in 2010 found that one in twelve pupils provide mid-level to high-level care for someone in their family. In Sheffield this means that Sheffield Young Carers estimate that we have over 7000 young carers in the city. This would be an average of just over 40 per school if they were spread evenly across all sectors.

'Young carers are in secondary schools'

The majority of young carers are found in secondary schools, but it is a smaller majority than you might think. Barnados say that the average age of a young carer is twelve. Our local data suggests that around 40% of the new referrals last year were aged twelve or under at the point of referral. It is dangerous to extrapolate this data too far, as this may simply reflect a greater awareness or identification of young carers at secondary age, but if only 20% of the estimated number of young carers in Sheffield were in a primary school this would be an average of more than ten per school.

We should also remember that the point of referral doesn't always reflect the age at which caring began. Whilst sometimes the point of referral coincides with a change of circumstance and is the point when a child begins taking on caring responsibilities, often young carers are not identified or offered support until the caring role comes to light due to a crisis or if a significant concern arises. The caring has often been happening for a long time before this, with the impacts already entrenched.

Given that young carers are also found across socio-economic groups and have a broad range of contextual factors, it isn't hard to reach the conclusion that there will be few schools who actually don't currently have any young carers.

If further food for thought was needed here about the under-identification of this group, a survey in 2010 found that 39% of young carers said that nobody in their school was aware of their caring role (The Princess Royal Trust for Carers).

What approach do schools need to take?

Once a school has recognised that they are likely to have young carers then a whole school approach to identifying and supporting young carers needs to be developed. The Carers Trust (see link below) suggest that all school staff need to have the knowledge and confidence to support young carers because:

- One of the main reasons young carers say they do not access support is stigma. A positive whole school ethos where young carers and their families are respected and valued by pupils, staff and the wider school community is crucial to ensuring young carers and their families feel safe and confident to access support.

- Many young carers are hidden. All school staff need to know how to identify young carers to ensure they do not slip through the net.

- A pupil with caring responsibilities may self-identify to any member of staff whom they feel they can talk to and share their worries and concerns.

- All staff need to be aware of the school's process for sharing information about a young carer. This will help ensure that information is only shared with the appropriate consent and with a view to guaranteeing that a pupil does not have to repeat their story several times.

- All staff should know not to discuss a pupil's caring role in front of their peers.

The identification and support of young carers is one of our Sheffield Priorities. We are working with Sheffield Young Carers on a pilot to explore approaches to identifying young carers in a group of primary schools. Initial findings suggest that this is difficult when the children involved do not already have some awareness of the concept of being a carer. It has also highlighted, perhaps predictably, the difficulties associated with introducing anything new into already busy organisations. More positively, we are seeing schools with strong existing provision, systems and culture for vulnerable pupils able to move relatively quickly to broaden this to identify and support young carers.

All of this suggests three initial steps for the school that wants to develop provision for young carers, to create the platform from which great provision can be developed.

1. Staff training needs to ensure that all staff have the knowledge to identify and support young carers.

2. School systems which relate to vulnerable learners need to be widened to include young carers, taking account of the advice above.

3. Awareness of the issues relating to young carers needs to be raised across the school community, as a first step towards developing a positive, safe and supportive culture for young carers.

Where can I find out more?

- The 'Carers Trust – Professionals' webpage links to useful sites and documents, including 'Step 1: Gaining and understanding about young carers'

professionals.carers.org (young carers are one of the categories)
professionals.carers.org/step-by-step-guide-gaining-an-understanding-about-young-carers

- The Children's Society report 'Hidden from view' describes the experience of being a young carer.
www.childrenssociety.org.uk/sites/default/files/hidden_from_view_final.pdf

- Sheffield Young Carers are a brilliant example of a local resources, and also have a section for professionals on their website.
www.sheffieldyoungcarers.org.uk/

- Keep an eye out for 'Young Carers Awareness Day' (January), 'Carers Week' (June) and 'Carers Rights Day' (Nov), which can provide easy opportunities to bring focus to this topic!

Stephen Betts, Learn Sheffield

Stephen is the Chief Executive of Learn Sheffield, which is a not-for-profit schools company owned by the schools and colleges of Sheffield, along with Sheffield City Council. He was previously a primary headteacher.

@LearnSheffield

Afterword

After a career in education that now dates back 45 years, I feel I have earned the right to be an old bore. So when Marc asked me if I'd read a book he was working on and provide some thoughts I couldn't resist the temptation to induce more stifled yawns. In the event, this thought-provoking collection took me down memory lane and got me reflecting on various events where I felt flickers of recognition, or even guilt.

The first of these was remembering when, as a young head of languages in a comprehensive school, I appointed a newly qualified teacher called Mike. He was very enthusiastic, read everything I gave him and applied the ideas rigorously. One of his classes was a Year 7 group with ten pupils who had special needs. I watched him teach them and he was systematic, demanding and somewhat fierce. Later, I took in their books to see how they were doing, and was horrified. He was getting a much higher standard of work in their written French than I was.

I thought hard about this, and realised that the main reason was that he had no prior expectation of what they could do. He just assumed that they should all be able to write neatly and accurately, so they did. And whenever they didn't, he kept them in until they did, a hard but productive discipline. For me, it was what is now called a 'learning curve'. I realised that, without knowing it, I'd trained my fleas to jump the height of the box I'd placed over them (thank you Kate Masters for that wonderful image), while his fleas were free-range, prodigious jumpers. I'd let the label create the limit.

A second epiphany came when, in my second year of teaching, I was working with a boy called Stephen in a Year 10 European Studies class. We worked slowly through a text and, via question and answer, he told me the gist of what he had read, eventually summarising it in two sentences. I praised him and said I now wanted him to write down what he had said. I went off to work with others in the class and returned ten minutes later. He had written a sentence, not totally correct but comprehensible. I asked him to read it out to me… and found he couldn't. Discovering that he couldn't read what he had written a few minutes before cut straight through the assumptions I had made about the barriers he faced.

I reached two conclusions about this experience. From now on, I would focus much more closely on individuals and what their problems were. Secondly, I had the strong feeling that it was not acceptable for a child to have reached Year 10 without any clear diagnosis of his difficulties or proper responses to them. We now talk about early intervention, but sadly I still often find that we talk about it more than we practise it. Crucial time is often lost, particularly in the early years, when a teacher's certain knowledge that a child needs help is not followed by rapid action from those services best placed to provide it. I remember an inspirational special needs coordinator in a large north-east primary school who told me that if a child was still 'on the register' by Key Stage 2 she believed she had failed.

Norman, an adult who couldn't read, is a fine example of late intervention. He was the last of nine children to go through his school, and because all of his siblings were 'problems', it was assumed that he would be as well. But he was a quiet lad, and because he didn't fight or break windows or cause trouble no-one really noticed him. No one taught him to read either. My wife did, inspired by a BBC adult literacy programme called 'On the Move'. He learned to read functionally but had no background, and therefore no interest, in reading for pleasure. He didn't understand the concept. So he never moved beyond the simple, functional level, and we probably learned more from him than he did from us.

We found that, as a jobbing builder, he'd turned up at a house one day to find a note left for him. He could recognise most of the individual letters, so he rang his wife and dictated them down the phone. She then read the message back to him. Vulnerable, but resourceful! We also discovered that he couldn't shop, because, unless there was a picture, he didn't know what was in the packets and tins. And he couldn't travel beyond the district, because he couldn't read the road signs or a map. We finally understood how life-limiting illiteracy is.

The seminal Bullock Report appeared in 1975 with its wonderful slogan: 'every teacher is a teacher of English'. For a few years, 'language across the curriculum' was the biggest show in town, but then, in true British fashion, it was placed on a back burner and simmered its way into virtual oblivion. When it was first published, we had an in-service training day at school, where we were told that the biggest weakness in education was in the development of spoken language. We failed to work on building vocabulary systematically, we failed to require pupils to speak at length, we failed to use the spoken language as a vehicle to explore ideas or to improve writing.

Sad to say, I feel that 40 years on we still fail to emphasise speaking sufficiently. Several articles in this book stress the importance of making language learning and development a key priority. This is not just because of its intrinsic value in supporting learning, but also because it builds confidence, articulacy and the ability to function well in society.

Many of the other articles in this book were familiar travellers on my trip down memory lane. The spike in exclusions when pupils go to secondary school is one of them. Do we consider how to help a 'difficult' Year 6 child who has struggled to adjust to the demands of one teacher, to suddenly cope in Year 7, with the demands of a dozen? "Oh dear", we used to say, "he won't last ten minutes at the comp".

What are the implications of being a 'looked after child', or a child with mental health difficulties? It would appear that one of the main ones is to have a vastly increased risk of spending a life in custody. How closely do we work with youth services, given that pupils spend a greater amount of time out of school than in it?

How do we support parents to become partners in their children's learning? Many of them have had a really poor experience of school themselves and have an often unrecognised phobia about stepping inside one. A headteacher once told me that she had invited into school a small group of parents of children soon to start in the Reception class. After a few minutes, a father had timidly raised his hand and said: "Please Miss, can I go to the toilet?". What courage had he needed to turn up at school in the first place?

This book poses all these challenges and more. Vulnerability comes in many forms, and responses to it require imagination and determination. There is a famous Peter Cook and Dudley Moore sketch where Sir Arthur Streeb-Greebling, an eccentric scientist, has spent all his time trying to teach cormorants to dance underwater. His life, as he admits, has been a complete failure, but he's not disposed to give up. Although his particular task seems futile (he hadn't assessed his pupils' needs!), he exemplifies an attitude that runs through this book: 'no they can't...yet'. The same sentiment was expressed in a different way by a group of pupils I interviewed once about why their inner-city school was succeeding against the odds. One summed it up simply and beautifully: "the teachers don't give up on you". The contributions and practical ideas in this book illustrate that mindset perfectly. It's what Ofsted inspectors call 'high expectations'.

Harmer Parr

Harmer Parr is a retired HMI. He now works as an adviser to the Department for Education.

Further Reading

Books

Rowland, Marc, 'An Updated Guide to the Pupil Premium', John Catt Educational Ltd, 2015.

Dunford, John, 'The School Leadership Journey', John Catt Educational Ltd, 2016.

Dweck, Carol, 'Mindset', Robinson, 2012.

Hymer, Barry, 'Growth Mindset Pocketbook', Teachers' Pocketbooks, 2014.

Syed, Matthew, 'Black Box Thinking: Marginal Gains and the Secret of High Performance', John Murray, 2016.

Syed, Matthew, 'Bounce' The Myth and Talent of the Power of Practice', Fourth Estate, 2011.

Webster, Rob, 'Maximising the Impact of Teaching Assistants' Routledge, 2015.

Gedge, Nancy, 'Inclusion for Primary School Teachers', Bloomsbury Education, 2016.

O'Brien, Jarlath, 'Don't Send Him in Tomorrow', Independent Thinking Press an imprint of Crown House Publishing 2016.

Myatt, Mary, 'High Challenge, Low Threat: How the Best Leaders Find the Balance', John Catt Educational Ltd, 2016.

Bauby, Jean-Dominique, 'The Diving Bell and the Butterfly', HarperCollins, 2008.

Peacock, Alison, 'Creating Learning Without Limits', Open University Press, 2012.

The Students of Limpsfield Grange School, 'M is for Autism', Jessica Kingsley Publishers, 2015.

Field, Frank, 'The Foundation Years: Preventing Poor Children Becoming Poor Adults', Stationery Office – Independent Review on Poverty and Life Chances for HM Government, 2010.

Websites

epi.org.uk/comment/progress-childrens-mental-health/, 'PROGRESS in Children's mental Health', April 2016

www.netacademies.net/raising-the-wellbeing-agenda-in-primary-schools/, 'Raising the Wellbeing Agenda in Primary Schools', January 2017

Syed, Matthew, 'Bounce: The Myth and Talent of the Power of Practice', Fourth Estate, 2011.

Webster, Rob, 'Maximising the Impact of Teaching Assistants', Routledge, 2015.

Gedge, Nancy, 'Inclusion for Primary School Teachers', Bloomsbury Education, 2016.

O'Brien, Jarlath, 'Don't Send Him in Tomorrow', Independent Thinking Press an imprint of Crown House Publishing 2016.

Myatt, Mary, 'High Challenge, Low Threat: How the Best Leaders Find the Balance', John Catt Educational Ltd, 2016.

Bauby, Jean-Dominique, 'The Diving Bell and the Butterfly', HarperCollins, 2008.

Peacock, Alison, 'Creating Learning Without Limits', Open University Press, 2012.

The Students of Limpsfield Grange School, 'M is for Autism', Jessica Kingsley Publishers, 2015.

Field, Frank, 'The Foundation Years: Preventing Poor Children Becoming Poor Adults', Stationery Office – Independent Review on Poverty and Life Chances for HM Government, 2010.

Websites

cpi.org.uk/common/progress-childrens-mental-health, 'PROGRESS in Children's mental Health', April 2016

www.netacademies.net/raising-the-wellbeing-agenda-in-primary-schools/, 'Raising the Wellbeing Agenda in Primary Schools', January 2017